A Grim Almanac of
GLOUCESTERSHIRE

A funerary statue in Leckhampton churchyard.

A Grim Almanac of GLOUCESTERSHIRE

ROBIN BROOKS

SUTTON PUBLISHING

Sutton Publishing Limited
Phoenix Mill · Thrupp · Stroud
Gloucestershire · GL5 2BU

First published 2004

Copyright © Robin Brooks, 2004

Title page photograph: Tombs in the churchyard at Painswick.

British Library Cataloguing in Publication Data
A catalogue record for this book is available from the British Library.

ISBN 0-7509-3538-3

Typeset in 10.5/13.5 Photina.
Typesetting and origination by
Sutton Publishing Limited.
Printed and bound in England by
J.H. Haynes & Co. Ltd, Sparkford.

The Grim Almanacs
are from an original idea by Neil R. Storey

CONTENTS

Leckhampton churchyard.

INTRODUCTION

If you are a sensitive soul, which no doubt you are, dear reader, you will notice while browsing this compilation of macabre misery, wanton wickedness and the murky underside of misfortune, that there are different categories of grimness. Sometimes, it seems, Lady Fate doesn't simply point her fickle finger at an unfortunate soul. She jabs them full in the eye.

Take the case of Penelope Noel, whose memorial on the wall of Chipping Campden church tells us she left this life in 1633. The sweet young thing pricked her finger while embroidering and shortly after died from blood poisoning. Who could ever have imagined that needlepoint could be a potentially fatal pastime?

Many more victims of death by the longest odds imaginable are recorded here. Gloucestrian John Stafford Smith, composer of the ponderous tune eventually adopted by the USA as its national anthem, was one minute cheerfully chewing on a grape and the next choking to death when the pip became lodged in his windpipe. We can only guess how many more memorable melodies he might have penned had seedless varieties been available at his local fruiterer. Bad luck with a particularly malicious twist was suffered by a navvy, one of hundreds digging out the Sapperton canal tunnel, who happened to be at the foot of a ventilation shaft when he was despatched by a box of earth falling on him, which his brother accidentally dropped from the top.

Some of these grim tales will tug at the heart strings. At Apperley stands the memorial to five young men killed in the First World War who were all members of the same family. From the Second World War comes the equally harrowing story of two children evacuated from the Midlands who were killed in the only bombing raid suffered by Painswick.

Then there are the examples of grimness at its most yucky: sanitary affairs, for instance. In 1372 Gloucester monks protested that effluent in the Fullbrook ponged so strongly that it put them off their prayers. Four centuries later a report on Cheltenham's sewerage arrangements revealed that there were none to speak of, so the problem of town-centre streets streaming with urine must have been almost as severe then as it is on most Friday and Saturday nights now. A similar lack of provision plagued Tewkesbury, where all the latrines emptied into the Avon. And guess where the town's main source of water was?

Grim, yet intriguing too, is the story of Winchcombe farmer John Lucas who, on discovering the lead coffin of Catherine Howard, fifth wife of Henry VIII and beheaded in 1542, thought he would prise off the lid and have a look. (If we are honest, this is sort of understandable.)

Public sensibilities to grimness change over time. When Eli Hatton was hanged in 1732 and his body left to rot in chains, there was such vociferous outcry that the corpse was removed by the authorities, not because anyone minded on moral grounds but because the remains attracted so many flies that local butchers were worried it would make their meat go off.

Grimness is, of course, the bedfellow of death. But life can be a pretty grim business for some, Mr and Mrs Ball, for instance, who in 1908 became parents to triplets, which brought their tally of children to seven. Mr Ball, a farm worker, earned 14*s* (that's 70p) a week. And as if that were not hardship enough, the local newspaper that told their story pointed out that the family lived 'just at the entrance to the corporation sewerage farm'.

Newspapers have always taken perverse pleasure in reporting the grimmer nooks of human misfortune. In the nineteenth century, however, they did so with particular relish and many words. One reason for this was that photographs did not appear until about 1900, so instead of picturing disasters, murderers, ravages of pestilence and so on, such mishaps were described in exhaustive verbal detail. If, for example, Thomas Pilkington Esq. passed on today, his obituary would probably comprise a portrait and caption. In 1861, however, the *Cheltenham Examiner* pulled out all the stops:

> We feel, while making this announcement, that it affords the subject for posthumous eulogy. During a residence of more than a quarter of a century in Cheltenham Mr. Pilkington has endeared himself to the hearts of thousands amongst us by the force of his character, the integrity of his principles, by the kindness of his disposition, by his conduct as a magistrate and private citizen, and by unnumbered acts of private and public munificence. Of his loss it may truly be said that 'Take him for all in all, We ne'er shall look upon his like again' and the public funeral, which is this day accorded to his remains, will be no mere idle pageant, but the 'outward and visible sign' of that deep sorrow at his loss which pervades the hearts of every class of his fellow-townsmen.

Of course, for grimness at its most concentrated, you can't beat an execution. And for a hard-hitting account of such an occasion it is difficult to top the eyewitness at Bishop Hooper's burning in Gloucester, who wrote, 'When he was black in the mouth and his tongue swollen, [so] that he could not speak, yet his lips went till they were shrunk to the gums, and he knocked his breast with his hands until one of his arms fell off, and then still knocked with the other, what time the fat, water and blood, dropped at his finger ends' . . . and so it goes on.

Putting aside the mental image those words conjure, let us take a concluding glimpse at yet another kind of grimness, the sort we might call grim, yet somehow inspiring. An obvious contender for the prize here is Captain Scott's ill-fated Antarctic expedition of 1912. After losing to Norway in the race to the South Pole, the party (which included Cheltonian Edward Wilson) battled appalling weather conditions, ran low on food and fuel and fell victim to frostbite; one died of concussion, another walked off to certain suicide and the remaining three froze to death just a few miles from safety. Grim? Yes. But it is a story that has swelled British hearts with pride for almost a century.

So is it true to suppose that we are less fascinated by the grim than we once were? Well, we do not have public executions anymore, but if we did, do you think there would be any free seats in the audience? How many times have you been stuck in a tailback on the M5 caused by traffic slowing for a peek at the accident? And, come to that, have you ever seen the tabloid headline 'Everything's great!'? Our taste for grimness, we may be sure, gentle reader, is with us to stay.

JANUARY

✟

There's a bricked-up doorway beneath the old railway bridge at the Gloucester Road end of Cheltenham High Street. According to the lore of the town's primary school playgrounds in years gone by, that doorway was once the entrance to a mortuary where the bodies of people who died in a plague were stored – and the entrance was sealed to prevent the plague getting out. Fanciful though this may sound, there may well be a grain of truth in the story, since this was in fact the entrance to High Street Halt, a railway station that closed during the First World War. The war ended in November 1918 and by cruel fate was followed by an influenza epidemic of such extraordinary ferocity that by January 1919 all Europe was held in its grip. The epidemic eventually accounted for more deaths than the recently ceased hostilities. During this 'plague' Cheltenham's conventional mortuary facilities were unable to cope, and so, according to some, the vacant space beneath the former railway station was put to a more macabre use.

1 JANUARY   **1856**   A Privy Council order made it illegal to bury the dead in churchyards within the parish of Winchcombe. This followed a similar order passed the previous year that forbade burials inside churches. The grave problem of overcrowding had been noted by a visitor who was shown round St Peter's by the sexton and noted: 'The ground beneath the pavement of the church is said to be full of dead bodies, and the effluvia is occasionally most offensive.'

2 JANUARY   **1941**   Gloucester suffered its first casualties of the war. At 7 a.m. a single Luftwaffe plane flew low across the city and dropped two bombs. The first fell on Napier Street, the second on Montpellier. There were sixteen people killed in the raid and twenty-four injured, with seventeen houses, a garage and an office destroyed. A day later a large bomb was dropped on Massey Road, which razed five houses, leaving a crater 25ft across and 10ft deep.

One of the houses destroyed in the Napier Street raid was no. 23, home of the Withers family. The head of the household was struggling into his clothes when the explosion took place. He was blown right out of the house to land some distance away, but was not badly injured.

His daughter Vera, who worked at Compton's cuff and collar works, was a bride-to-be. Her fiancé was in the Royal Navy on Russian convoy duty, and the local vicar had agreed to marry the couple as soon as the young sailor was allowed home on leave. Vera's family pooled their clothing coupons for her wedding dress, which was hanging in the wardrobe when the bomb fell. It looked like Miss Withers' hopes of a white wedding had been dashed to smithereens – until the manager of the Bon Marché, then Gloucester's premier department store, read of her plight in the *Citizen* and supplied a new dress free of charge.

3 JANUARY   **1533**   Henry VIII and Anne Boleyn married secretly. This proved to be a mistake for Anne, as she was beheaded three years later. In the church of John the Baptist, Cirencester, a glass case at the entrance to the chancel contains an ornamental drinking cup that was made for Anne the year before she was dispatched. The lid is topped by her personal emblem of a falcon holding a sceptre with a rose tree.

When Anne was accused of adultery and executed, the cup passed to her daughter Elizabeth I, who in turn gave it to her physician Richard Master. He acquired the abbey lands after the dissolution of the monastery and gave the cup to the parish church.

4 JANUARY   **1967**   Donald Campbell was killed while making an attempt at the world water speed record on Coniston Water in the Lake District. For a time in the 1960s the speed ace worked for the local Dowty company, which acquired the rights to manufacture and market a jet-powered boat invented in New Zealand. Dowty Marine assumed responsibility for the project. Besides being fast, the jet boat could operate in very shallow water and was thought to have great potential for military and leisure uses. The company looked around for a high-profile personality to help publicise the venture, with the result that Donald Campbell became titular Managing Director of Dowty Marine.

1799   William Beames, who died on this day, is buried at Duntisbourne Abbots. His epitaph reads,

> A warning piece to all young men
> Who in their blooming age
> Mispend their time and know not when
> They must go off the stage.

5 JANUARY

1630   At the west end of Gloucester Cathedral you will find a monument to John Jones Esq. – three times Mayor of Gloucester – who died on this day. As was the custom for luminaries at the time, Jones commissioned his own monument. At each stage of its making he inspected and approved the work, or sometimes did not approve it. The artist responsible for painting the statue was sternly rebuked, for example, for making the Jones nose too red. When the monument was completed to his satisfaction, Mr Jones paid off the craftsmen – just in time, as he died next day.

6 JANUARY

Dickie Dumpling, diminutive boot boy at the Bell Hotel, Gloucester, died in January 1908.

1936   Gloucester's premier department store, the Bon Marché, was selling clothes, furnishings, household items, fancy goods . . . and aeroplanes. For £85 you could walk into the store and buy a Flying Flea, designed by a Frenchman named Mignet.

The tiny craft measured 13ft in length and had a 27ft wingspan. It weighed 230lb, was capable of 75mph and returned a respectable 50 miles to the gallon. With a range of 200 miles and the ability to land virtually anywhere, the Flying Flea looked destined to be a great success – until a design fault was noticed, with fatal consequences. Put simply, the Flea was a killer. It was impossible to pull the minuscule microplane out of a dive and a number of pilots died before the Flying Flea was banned. An example of this novel, but lethal little aircraft can be seen at the Brooklands Museum in Weybridge.

7 JANUARY

1930   By now the condition of housing in the Westgate area of Gloucester had become a disgrace to the city. The back-to-backs were each without water, sewerage, or mains facilities of any kind. Instead, residents had to share a stand-pipe and outside lavatory. To make matters worse, the area was prone to regular flooding. It was widely acknowledged that the slums needed to be cleared, but the council, claiming poverty, could not raise sufficient funds.

When violent storms in January 1930 tore through Westgate, a writer with the *Gloucestershire Graphic* took the opportunity to focus local minds on the plight of people who lived in that quarter: 'When not being invaded by floods, this slum area has been lashed by the force of 100mph gales. Small wonder

8 JANUARY

that its population goes about with anxious eyes. Last week's gale hit them very hard indeed. Several roofs were stripped of slates and windows blown in.

'Those houses in Westgate – some of them built over 100 years ago – are none too substantial and a repetition of this year's weather would probably raze them to the ground. Perhaps that would be a good thing. The authorities do not like the idea of pulling them down, so perhaps the elements will do the job for them.'

9 JANUARY   **1614**   A Gloucestershire rector, the Revd R.W. Hippisley, recorded in his journal that on this day 'began the greatest snow which ever fell upon the earth within men's memory. It covered the earth five quarters deep.' A quarter was 9in – i.e. a quarter of a yard – making the snowfall 3ft 9in in depth.

Twenty years later, snow fell continuously for three weeks. It was accompanied by violent storms of wind, which caused considerable damage to houses, and many people perished on county highways. The summer that followed was noted for its extreme heat, yet so thick was the snow and ice of the preceding winter that large quantities of it remained unthawed at the quarries of Brockhampton.

10 JANUARY   **1945**   At the end of the Second World War, Great Western warehouse near Llanthony Bridge in Gloucester was a factory employing about forty people who produced breakfast cereals. A dust explosion in an oak hopper caused a fire, which spread rapidly and was soon out of control, as flames leaped 150ft into the air.

The docks' fire boat *Salamander* was brought into action, but in the heat of the moment was not properly anchored before its powerful water jets were activated. The fire boat spun round and, instead of quenching the factory fire, its hoses soaked the crowd of onlookers gathered at the dockside. After some hours the inferno died down, but not before the upper part of the building had been destroyed.

The fire boat *Salamander* in Gloucester docks.

1778 Snow falling fast and furiously embedded for seventy-two hours a convoy of three wagons travelling from Cheltenham to Tewkesbury. Then, in 1793, a convoy of three wagons set off from Cheltenham bound for Tewkesbury and became trapped in another snowstorm of great violence. The drivers and horses all perished.

1874 Gloucester prison was the venue for a triple execution. Hanged on that day were Charles Butt, Edwin Bailey and Anne Barry. The prosecution explained that Butt had shot the woman who was his next-door neighbour, because she refused to accompany him to Gloucester cheese fair.

Edward Bailey and Anne Barry were accused of poisoning a child. Its mother, Miss Susan Jenkins, had claimed that Bailey was the father. Bailey had then encouraged his accomplice, Anne Barry, who was working as the child's nanny, to poison the child with strychnine.

Condemned prisoners arriving at Gloucester gaol made their last journey in a Black Maria.

While the three guilty prisoners awaited their fate a crowd gathered at the GWR railway station to catch a glimpse of the celebrated hangman Mr Calcraft, known as 'Old Cal'. They were disappointed, as Old Cal – at the age of 78 – did not consider himself up to the task of a triple hanging and so sent Mr Anderson, his younger assistant, instead.

Perhaps due to inexperience, Anderson did not bring sufficient rope for the dispatch of three, so a prison messenger and ex-seaman named Barnaby was commissioned to make a stretch of sufficient length overnight.

Fifty people witnessed the gruesome spectacle, which took place in the prison yard. Three nooses were strung from a crossbeam, and beneath the trapdoor a deep pit had been excavated. At 08.04 on that cold morning the condemned trio left their cells for the last time.

The Tomb of Robert, Duke of Normandy, Gloucester

13 JANUARY   1940   Unlike Canterbury Cathedral's stained glass, which was removed and stored during the Second World War, Gloucester's wonderful Crecy window at the east end of the nave remained in place – and mercifully suffered no damage. By bad luck, however, as befits this day of the month, the cathedral lost one of its treasures in the war. Just before hostilities were declared, a sixteenth-century altarpiece depicting the Day of Judgment was sent to London for restoration – where it was destroyed in the Blitz.

14 JANUARY   1675   On one of four carved tablets set into the east wall of the transept in Ampney Crucis church is a memorial to the squire, Robert Pleydell, which pinpoints more accurately than most the moment when he shuffled off this mortal coil. He died on this day 'between the hours of 2 and 3 a.m., having lived for almost 58 years'.

15 JANUARY   1929   A goods train was travelling up the line from Ashchurch. Thick fog had reduced visibility, which could explain why the driver of an oncoming passenger train overran the signal. When the Bristol–Leeds express collided at full speed with the goods train a scene of mangled devastation resulted. Locals in Tewkesbury clearly heard the crash, and with daylight the full horrifying extent of the accident became apparent. The driver of the express, a man from Derby named Crabtree, was killed, but amazingly no others were injured. It took nine days to clear the tons of debris.

TERRIBLE TRAIN TRAGEDY AT ASHCHURCH STATION.

On Tuesday evening last, about 9 o'clock, the express train on the L.M.S. Railway, which had just left Cheltenham for Birmingham, Derby, and the North, crashed into a goods train which was being shunted across the main lines at Ashchurch Station. The Mail train was travelling at close on 50 miles per hour, and a terrible smash occurred, the whole train being derailed, the engine thrown on its side, and the carriages piled upon and around it in inextricable confusion. Four persons were killed outright and twenty injured. Our pictures were taken as soon as it was light the next morning.

1.—Clearing the debris on the down line, the roof of one of the mail vans is shown in centre.   3.—All that was left of the chassis of one of the wrecked carriages: the buffers can be seen
2.—The tender of the express engine (shown by arrow) is protruding from the wreckage, the   at each end.
      engine itself is buried.

1852   There was reported a 'Dreadful accident to Master Findon, only son of Mr. Findon, of Prestbury. Deceased, who was only 15 years of age, was following the hounds and on taking a fence his horse swerved and threw him onto some sharp stakes in the hedge, by which he received such serious injuries as to cause his death'.

16 JANUARY

Young hunter was for the high jump.

17 JANUARY **1913** Eighteen-year-old Sidney Coleman (right) and a friend were killed under Arle Road railway bridge, Cheltenham by a passing train.

18 JANUARY **1933** Cheltenham's slum clearance programme meant that this month residents of Swindon Passage left their meagre homes for the last time.

Swindon Place, which stood where the Post Office sorting office in the Lower High Street stands today, was a terrace of twenty-eight back-to-back houses built in the 1820s to accommodate the town's labouring and unemployed classes. Three earth-closet privies were shared – along with the squalor – by all.

As early as 1849 Swindon Place was described by a Board of Health inspector as being 'without sewerage, carriageway or pavement: the gutter channels on the surface are always full of filthy fluid; and the place is never free from fever. Wanting in ventilation, the houses are always in an unhealthy condition'. Each house had a flagstone-floored living room 14ft square in which was a hearth and oven. Upstairs were two small bedrooms. Not one of the houses had a bathroom, a few had mains water from a tap under the stairs, but most shared a communal pump. The rent in 1930 was *6s 6d* a week.

19 JANUARY **1941** Amy Johnson rose to celebrity when she became the first woman to fly solo from England to Australia. She lived in Stoke Orchard, near Bishops Cleeve, and on this day was killed in an air accident while a pilot for the Air Transport Auxiliary.

20 JANUARY **1801** In this largely agricultural county, pest control has long been taken very seriously. As in other towns and villages, a bounty on vermin killed was paid by the churchwardens of St Peter's church, Winchcombe, out of the tithe fund. In the mid-eighteenth century a shilling was paid for every fox's head brought to the vestry 'to be cut in sunder or otherwise destroyed'. Until the middle of the nineteenth century a farthing was paid for each sparrow's head, and the records reveal that these birds were far more abundant than they are now. The churchwardens doled out *16s 1d 3f* for 775 decapitated sparrows.

21 JANUARY **1840** A highway robbery and attempted murder was reported at Piff's Elm near Coombe Hill. A man named Yarworth was travelling the route when he was shot by a footpad and left for dead. The miscreant was not apprehended.

22 JANUARY **1787** The *Gloucester Journal* reported a fatal accident involving a navvy engaged on the Sapperton Tunnel stretch of the Thames and Severn canal. 'In the prosecution of this work, many men have lost their lives. One man was killed a few days ago by the carelessness of his companion, who suffered one of the boxes used in drawing the earth up the shafts, to fall down into the pit, which killed the person at the bottom. The men were brothers.'

1852 *Cheltenham Examiner:* 'Loss of the *Amazon*, West Indian steamer. She left Southampton with 161 souls on board and when off the Scilly Islands was discovered to be on fire. Forty-six persons saved themselves in the boats, but the remaining 115 were either drowned or burned. Among the sufferers was Mr. Rycroft Best, a gentleman long residing in Cheltenham and who was making a last visit to the West Indies to dispose of his property. He was accompanied by an old and faithful servant named Chute, who shared his master's fate. Mrs. Best and her family, and poor Chute's wife and three children, were in Cheltenham when news of the catastrophe arrived and their bereavement called forth a universal expression of sorrow and sympathy.'

23 JANUARY

1585 In the days when brewing was a craft, rather than an industry, Gloucester boasted numerous small brewers. One such was Alderman John Thorne (1545–1618), who lived near St Nicholas's church in Westgate Street. Where his brewery was is not recorded, but we do know that one of the employees, Walter Trigge, had the misfortune to die at the premises by falling into a vat of boiling water.

24 JANUARY

1990 Early in the 1960s a ragged looking character in his mid-forties arrived on the outskirts of Swindon Village. His name was Cyril Kingman – though he liked to be called Charlie – and smoke seen curling from the spinney at the end of Dog Bark Lane announced that he had taken up residence.

25 JANUARY

Charlie remained part of – but also apart from – the Swindon Village community for the next thirty years. His first home was a bivouac of polythene sheets and corrugated iron tacked over a timber frame. A pile of sacks made his bed, and the only furniture to clutter up the place was an oak stump, which served as a table. It was not an interior designer's dream come true, but then the smoke rising lazily from the open fire inside the shelter pretty well obscured what little there was to look at.

A few pots and pans hung from trees around and about, and Charlie's washing arrangements were found conveniently nearby in the shape of Wyman's Brook (the stream, not the housing estate). Sharing this rural idyll was Jack, the Jack Russell (a dog, not the wicket-keeper).

Gradually the village took Charlie under its wing. When his bivouac burned down, a few villagers got together and built him a wooden shack. And rather than do the conventional thing and be grateful, Charlie forever after complained that his old bivouac of polythene sheets had been warmer.

Over the years rumours and facts about Charlie's past became one and the same. He was a former pupil of Lydney grammar school who served for three years in the Royal Navy during the war. He'd also been a professional gardener on a number of well-to-do estates and at Prinknash Abbey. He said that he had been dismissed from his job at the local monastery because he stole something from the shop. If that was true, the monks clearly did not hold the misdemeanour against Charlie, as once or twice a year they used to come and collect him and take him back to Prinknash for a holiday.

In 1990 Charlie was found in the field where he had collapsed, curious cows gathered round him. He was taken to Cheltenham General Hospital where he died aged 76. In the pocket of his well-worn tweed jacket was a bundle wrapped in newspaper containing over £1,000 in cash, with a note explaining that this was to pay for his funeral.

26 JANUARY **1777** Hangings took place on the common in Cheltenham in centuries past, the common then known as the Marsh, on which Pittville now stands. The land was crossed by Gallows Lane, which ran out to Prestbury. In this year a Cheltenham footman named Joseph Armstrong poisoned his employer, who had discovered him stealing. Armstrong was found guilty of murder and hanged at the county gaol. Then his body was returned to Cheltenham and hung in chains on a gibbet that had been erected on the Marsh – but not very well, because the gibbet collapsed and Armstrong's body fell to the ground. A local tradesman had to be hired to repair the structure.

The body was left on public view for a year, then the skull was bought by Dr Minster and the rest of the skeleton by Dr Newell, both Cheltenham physicians. The oak used to make the gibbet was acquired by the owner of Clonbrock House and recycled as gateposts.

27 JANUARY **1858** *Cheltenham Examiner*: 'On Sunday last, in the hamlet of Woodmancote, Ann Kitchen, aged 105, breathed her last. Deceased was formerly a market woman and as such attended Cheltenham weekly for many years. For the last two years, however, she had been bedridden, but possessed her faculties, both visual and intellectual, unimpaired up until the period of her death. Deceased was the oldest woman in the county.'

28 JANUARY **1854** *Gloucester County Directory* includes this informative advertisement: 'Whoever wants a clock repaired should apply to John Gardner. He is a Teetotaller of 30 years and also a herbalist who undertakes to cure the piles, fevers, small pox and cancers. John Gardner also has on sale a new and simple kind of truss for the accommodation of those who may need such things. Mrs. Gardner provides tea, coffee and good, cheap and cheerful beds.'

29 JANUARY **2000** Like other distinctive areas of Cheltenham, South Town has its resident ghost, who is said to walk abroad on dark January nights. The old man of St Phillip's Street, so the story goes, is sometimes seen in the narrow alley that runs behind the terrace of houses. Carrying a gas mask, he asks lone passers-by if they have seen his dog. The question asked, a distant barking is heard and the spectral figure vanishes. He was spotted on this day in the year 2000.

The haunted alley in St Phillip's Street, Cheltenham.

1649 Charles I was executed outside Whitehall Palace, London, an event that prompted some brutal tree surgery in Badgeworth, Gloucestershire. Richard Freeman, who owned a field adjacent to the churchyard in which grew a splendid oak, was an enthusiastic monarchist in the Civil War. He declared that if the king was not allowed to keep his head, neither was his tree, so he cut the crown from the trunk.

30 JANUARY

31 JANUARY **1773** In a letter, the Revd Winterbotham of Cheltenham wrote about the burial of two sisters who had been thought witches. 'These two women and their cat were certainly the terror of the neighbourhood. They subsisted by means of parochial aid and what they obtained by asking at the hands of their good neighbours who were afraid to refuse them anything while living, but who avenged themselves by refusing Christian interment to their mortal remains. I believe neither of them had even a coffin, at least I recollect seeing one of these innocent victims of folly with their clothes on dragged in a cart followed by a noisy rabble and buried in a piece of boggy ground without the town with less ceremony than has often attended the burial of a dog.'

The Gordon Lamp, Montpellier.

JANUARY **1885** In January of this year General Gordon was killed at Khartoum. Thinking an ornamental lamp standard might be a fitting memorial, residents in the Montpellier area of Cheltenham made a public appeal for funds, but just £20 trickled in. As the chosen light cost £200 the organisers had to make up the difference.

Then there was the question of who would bear the cost of illumination. The gas company quoted £22 per year, but the council said it couldn't pay more than £15 and suggested that only two of the three lamps should be lit.

There were other problems too. The granite base was late arriving. The ironwork wasn't strong enough and had to be modified. And further expense was incurred when the lamp was converted to electricity in 1900. Due to all the wrangling, nobody remembered to add a plaque commemorating General Gordon until 1933.

FEBRUARY

✠

Valentine's day falls this month; in times gone by the people of Minchinhampton celebrated this day by eating specially prepared pease pudding. How romantic! Shrove Tuesday is another February festival, immediately preceded by Collop Monday. Cause for another culinary delight, this was traditionally the day when Gloucestershire folk ate the remains of the bacon that had been preserved by salting during the previous autumn. It was an unfortunate month for Mrs Dormer, 'a lady well known in Cheltenham' as the Cheltenham Looker-On *reported in 1855, who 'died from injuries received from her dress coming in contact with the drawing room fire at her residence, 11, Lansdown Place'. The same newspaper informed its readers in February 1859 of the 'Suicide of Baron Philibert de Chastellain at the Eight Bells Inn by shooting himself in the stomach. Some monetary disarrangements, added to a love affair, were believed to be the cause of the rash act.'*

1 FEBRUARY **1939** A most serious landslide took place this month. At the time the runway at Brockworth aerodrome was being extended. A fleet of lorries ferried top-soil removed in these excavations to a dump near the quarries at Fiddler's Elbow. But the site had not been checked properly and lorry-loads of dumped earth dammed a stream running off the hill. Consequently an increasing weight of water was held back by a growing mass of soil and something had to give. It did. Conditions made worse by heavy rain caused land along a 500ft front to slip 30yd down the slope in one night. The A46 was closed and crowds gathered to watch as the slow, brown avalanche moved inexorably towards Pincott farmhouse. Forced to move by the approaching morass of semi-solid sludge, the farmer's family saw their home engulfed.

Pincott Farm engulfed by the landslide.

2 FEBRUARY **1880** An actress named Eliza Johnson appeared at Gloucester's Westgate Street Theatre Royal. While there she fell for the charms of Mr J.L. Toole, the theatre manager, but when he spurned her, Eliza took her own life in her dressing room.

In 1911 the theatre became a cinema. Then in 1922 the silver screen was removed and Woolworths moved in. In 1970 Woolies went and Texas took over, and it was six years later that customers in the do-it-yourself emporium spotted the ghostly figure of a Victorian woman, theatrical and distressed, on a stairway. The appearance was accompanied by a strong smell of burning.

When Texas made way for Poundsaver, workmen reported a distinct letter 'E' imprinted on the wall in the basement, which despite their best efforts would not be shifted.

Theatre Royal, Westgate Street (left) spooked by the spurned Eliza Johnson.

1938 On this day fishermen Jack Duffield, Edgar Bevan and Sidney Church, working a stretch of the Severn downstream from Haw, near Tirley, netted an

3 FEBRUARY

unexpected catch. It was the torso of an adult man, headless and limbless. Celebrated Home Office pathologist Sir Bernard Spilsbury arrived to examine the remains and dispatched organs to his London laboratory. Crowds of 5,000 gathered at Haw Bridge hoping dragging operations on the river would bring more gore to the surface – and they did: first an arm; then a leg; followed by another arm. The hands and foot had been severed. Enough of the body was now assembled to issue a limited description of the deceased. The dead man was mid-fifties, about 5ft 9in tall, and weighed

Fishermen at Haw Bridge netted a headless, limbless human torso.

MONDAY GLOUCESTERSHIRE ECHO FEBRUARY 7, 1938

MOTOR-CYCLIS FATAL CRASH

FAIRFORD INQUEST S: OF COLLISION WIT PEDAL CYCLE

A verdict of accidental was returned at the inque Cirencester on Saturday Kempsford, near Fairford, u cyclist.

The inquest was on William Ha jun., rate collector, who died in cester Memorial Hospital on Feb at the result of injuries receive his motor-cycle was in collision pedal-cycle ridden by Albert I Harding, general labourer, of F on the Fairford-Lechlade road a ford on February 2.

Harding was exonerated fro: blame.

The inquest was held by Dr. Ma deputy coroner for the Stroud (and a jury of whom Mr. Harry Pr foreman.

William Hayward, sen., of the low, Kempsford, said his son, who years of age and had been a rate tor employed by the Cirencester District Council, lived with him. left home at 12.30 p.m. on Wed (Feb. 2) on his motor-cycle an going to friends at Lechlade

The diver, Mr. Joseph Lane, at the back of the launch, about to start diving at Haw Bridge.

Divers discovered more body parts.

around 11 stone. Captain William Bernard Butt of Old Bath Road, Leckhampton, was reported missing. Captain Butt's description? He was in his mid-fifties, about 5ft 9in tall and weighed around 11 stone.

Among the missing man's possessions were found letters from Brian Sullivan, who had been found gassed three weeks earlier at Tower Lodge, Leckhampton. Beneath the flagstone floor police unearthed a heavily bloodstained overcoat belonging to Captain Butt. An axe with unidentified stains was removed from the lodge.

As the date of the Haw Bridge torso inquest loomed, efforts to find the missing head were redoubled, but no head was discovered. It was, therefore, a foregone conclusion that Coroner Mr R.D. Lane was forced to accept. 'The jury are unanimous on an open verdict on the body of an unidentified male person and as to the cause of death.'

The victim, Captain W.B. Butt of Leckhampton.

1278 As a child you may have sung 'Doctor Foster went to Gloucester in a shower of rain. He stepped in a puddle, right up to his middle and never went there again', but what is it all about?

4 February

The story goes that when King Edward I visited the city to proclaim the Statute of Gloucester (which declared that business could only be conducted with royal permission, and was a cunning way for the monarch to levy a new tax) his horse became stuck in the mud. Ever ready to see the funny side, Gloucester folk gathered to enjoy the free entertainment, as the King of England wallowed about in the mire. His Majesty, however, did not share the joke, and consequently vowed never to return to the city.

1912 Macabre events unfolded at the Park Grocery Stores, Cheltenham. Two elderly women, Mrs Davies and Mrs Barton, ran this local shop in Tivoli Street. It seems likely they chose not to spend any of the profits on home maintenance, as the windows were broken, the roof leaked and the entire building was damp and dank. Investigations were made when the shop remained shut for a few days and no sign was seen of its keepers. Both women were discovered inside, frozen to death. According to an *Echo* report of the time, one body was found 'nude on some flock in the kitchen and the other, also found in the kitchen, was wearing only an old black skirt'.

5 February

1802 Gloucester has its place in the history of communication. On this day Charles Wheatstone was born at Barnwood Manor. Wheatstone invented the telegraphic system, and was the first person in the world to send a telegram.

6 February

Wheatstone's invention shot to fame in 1845, when it made possible the apprehension of a murderer. The villain, dramatically dressed in a cloak, killed a woman in Slough, and was then seen to jump aboard a London-bound train. News of this event and a description of the felon were whizzed to Paddington along Wheatstone's wires. And when the murderer alighted from his carriage in the capital, the boys in blue were there to clap him in cuffs.

1914 When the west wing of Arle Court (now Cheltenham Film Studio) was set ablaze in this year, the *Gloucestershire Graphic* recorded: 'Despite the tempestuous weather, the inmates had to escape hurriedly in their night attire, three of the servants jumping from their bedroom window. One of them broke her arm and another injured her spine.'

7 February

Staff leaped from upper rooms in the Arle Court blaze.

8 February

The memorial to
Bishop Hooper,
Gloucester.

Right: Bishop
Hooper's final
lodgings, Westgate
Street, Gloucester

1555 John Hooper, the second Bishop of Gloucester, met a terrible end when he was burned at the stake in the city as a heretic. He spent the night in the Westgate Street house that is now the Folk Museum, then next morning a crowd of 7,000 gathered around St Mary's knapp, a small mound near St Mary de Lode church, where the execution was to take place. Hooper was bound to the stake with an iron hoop. Twice, the fire around him was lit, and twice it went out. More dry wood was brought and three bags of gunpowder were tied to Hooper's body, but they were ineffectual and Hooper was subjected to forty-five minutes in the flames, until he lost consciousness and died.

An eyewitness account describes his final moments: 'But when he was black in the mouth and his tongue swollen, that he could not speak, yet his lips went till they were shrunk to the gums, and he knocked his breast with his hands until one of his arms fell off, and then still knocked with the other, what time the fat, water and blood, dropped at his finger ends, until by renewing of the fire his strength was gone and his hand did cleave fast in knocking to the iron upon his breast. So, immediately bowing forwards, he yielded up his spirit.'

Bishop Hooper
burning at the stake.
He remained
conscious in the
flames for forty-five
minutes.

1604 Ann Parsons, a 16-year-old heiress, was married against her will to Anthony Palmer, who was after her money. Not surprisingly, the new Mrs Palmer went on to lead a desperately unhappy life and her ghost, limp and melancholic, is said to haunt Snowshill Manor.

Snowshill Manor, where the spirit of the unfortunate Ann Parsons is said to walk abroad.

1861 A hurricane ripped through Gloucester where, in the words of local historian John Goding, who was writing at the time, it brought 'about 40ft of the railway station down, the iron pillars being snapped asunder and the corrugated roof twisted like so much paper'.

1942 An American sergeant named Arn was on a training flight from Staverton with Flying Officer G.G. Pledger in a De Havilland Tiger Moth. The biplane collided with a Miles Master being flown by New Zealander S.C. Jones. Both planes came down at Pardwood Mansions in Shurdington Road, Cheltenham. There were no survivors.

1886 On the chancel wall of Great Barrington church is a tablet to the memory of Charles John Fitzroy Wingfield, Squire of Barrington Park and, we may assume, a keen angler.

> God grant that I may fish until my dying day.
> And when it comes to my last cast
> I humbly pray
> When in the Lord's safe landing net
> I'm peacefully asleep
> That in his mercy
> I be judged as good enough to keep.

1542 On this day Catherine Howard, the fifth wife of Henry VIII, was beheaded, leaving the way open for His Majesty to marry Katherine Parr, who eventually died and was buried in the chapel at Sudeley Castle. The Castle was slighted in the Civil War, and the chapel fell into ruin, but a century later the lead coffin of Henry's last spouse was discovered by John Lucas, a local farmer.

He opened the casket and found the body 'wrapp'd in 6 or 7 seer cloths of linnen entire and uncorrupted, although it had lain upward of 230 years'. A cut made in the cloths revealed the flesh still 'moist and white', but when Lucas took another look at the body a year later he discovered that 'where the incision had been made the flesh was brown and in a state of putrefaction'.

In 1792 Lucas and a party of drinking pals took the corpse from its coffin and 'made sport of it'. Within a short time, each of them suffered a horrible end.

14 FEBRUARY 1935 *The last reported occasion of an ancient superstition being carried out.* In a field to the north of Avening is a curiously pock-marked standing stone, pierced in places by wind and weather. Locally known by some as the Tingle Stone, by others as the Holey Stone, it has for centuries been thought to have healing powers. In time of yore the mothers of sickly children squeezed their offspring through a hole in the stone. This was believed magically to improve health, and to be particularly efficacious in the case of rickets.

15 FEBRUARY 1949 A stage hypnotist named Peter Casson appeared at Cheltenham Town Hall. Asking for a volunteer, Casson put his helper in a trance, then stuck pins through her hand. The volunteer felt no discomfort, but a man in the audience fainted at the sight, fell forward and broke his nose on the seat in front.

16 FEBRUARY 1857 *Cheltenham Examiner*: 'Accident to Earl Fitzhardinge. While following the hounds in the Vale of Berkeley, when his lordship was stooping to avoid an overhanging bough, the horse stumbled in a grip and the sudden check caused the rider to be thrown over the horse's head with considerable violence. His lordship, however, fortunately managed to pitch upon his shoulder. It was feared at first that one or more ribs had been broken. The carriage was sent for and the noble earl conveyed to Berkeley Castle and messengers despatched for medical assistance. It was hoped for some time that the noble earl had not sustained any serious injury. The shock to the system was, however, so great that he never recovered his usual health, but continued to gradually sink until the time of his death, which took place on Saturday evening in the 71st year of his age.'

17 FEBRUARY 1887 Hangings were conducted at Gloucester prison between the years of 1786 and 1939, during which time 140 miscreants were dispatched. According to the records, only two executions took place in the month of February. One was Edward Pritchard, aged 20, who on this day paid the penalty for murdering a 14-year-old boy in Stroud. The victim had just collected £186 from a bank for his employer when Pritchard attacked him with a billhook, grabbed the cash and ran.

Also hanged for murder was Herbert Burrows, a probationary police constable. While on duty this PC killed the landlord of a pub in Worcester, then murdered his wife and 2-year-old child too, before stealing £70. The 23-year-old Burrows was hanged on this day in 1926.

In Gloucester prison 132 men and eight women have been hanged. The youngest was 16-year-old John Baker, convicted of burglary in 1821. The oldest, John Evans, aged 70, was also convicted of burglary and sent to meet his maker in 1793.

17 FEBRUARY 1927 A fourth-generation Prestburyian recalled that February was a busy month for Daisybelle Little, the village's self-appointed director of funerals. No doubt she was good at her job, but it must be said that she lacked diplomacy:

'Poor old Daisybelle Little lived in Chapel Cottage by the chapel near the Apple Tree at Woodmancote. She used to go round laying people out. She came down because we were expecting my gramp to go, but he hadn't died. When he saw her, he said, "Here, I ain't dead yet!" She said, "All right then boss, I'll come back later."'

1843   *Cheltenham Examiner*: 'Attempted assassination of the Rev. R. Bennett, of Evington Cottage, Coombe Hill, by his wife and stepson. Mr. Bennet was a clergyman of independent fortune, possessing, it is said, £1,800 a year, and in consequence of some domestic quarrel, his wife's son shot him with a pistol, his wife assisting. Mother and son were committed for trial. On the trial at the ensuing assizes both prisoners were acquitted.'

19 FEBRUARY

1645   Sir Baptist Hicks was a prominent London merchant who won favour with James I by lending money to the monarch. In return the King granted Hicks 'our rectory and church at Cheltenham, our chapel at Charlton Kings and our church at Campden'. This made Hicks a powerful landowner in the area. To proclaim the fact, he built himself an impressive seat named Campden House, then burnt it down during the English Civil War for fear that it might fall into Parliamentarian hands. How he felt when Oliver Cromwell and company did not come near Chipping Campden we can only imagine, especially as the pile that Baptist Hicks torched must have been great and grand to judge by the lodges and gateway that remain to this day.

20 FEBRUARY

1861   *Cheltenham Examiner*: 'Great hurricane in Cheltenham. The first storm broke over the town at about 11 o'clock on the night of the 20th and the wind blew with uncontrollable fury until about 3 o'clock on the morning of the 21st. In the morning the town presented a scene of widespread desolation. Trees were uprooted and broken in every direction; chimnies blown down; houses partially unroofed; and windows forced in, on Bayshill, Lansdown and all the more exposed situations.

21 FEBRUARY

'In the High Street shutters were wrenched from their fastenings and whirled several hundred yards through the streets; and many of the shopkeepers were obliged to keep watch and ward over their premises until the cessation of the storm, or the approach of daylight.

'In the Christ Church district the church itself had several hundred panes of glass broken; a row of houses just finished in the Malvern Road were unroofed and the walls cracked and twisted in every direction. At Aban Court two chimney stacks were blown down as also were two at Suffolk Hall, the bricks of one falling completely through the roof and into a bedroom (fortunately unoccupied) beneath.

'Two of the noble elms in the Old Wells Drive were destroyed and several others much injured. At Hatherley Court a conservatory was carried bodily away and a large number of plants destroyed; the drawing room window was also blown in and a large mirror thrown from one end of the room to the other.

'At the corner of Henrietta Street, stones to the weight of two tons from the house of Mr. Booth, draper, were hurled into the middle of the road. To enumerate the instances of similar damage in other parts of the town would occupy too much space; suffice it to say that chimney stacks were blown down and roofs wholly or partially destroyed in nearly every district.

'Among the more serious casualties may be mentioned the fall of the chimnies at Mr. Maillard's, Gloucester Place, by which the bedrooms were almost filled with the ruins and several of the inmates severely injured.

'In a small cottage near Lord Dunalley's a high chimney was toppled over and several tons of debris fell into a bedroom in which four people were sleeping. The escape of the inmates was almost miraculous; the bricks and beams lay piled up in every part of the room higher than the bed itself, yet the bed and the four persons sleeping upon it escaped injury. On the following afternoon (the 21st) about 5 o'clock the storm returned in all its fury, but fortunately it only lasted about half an hour, yet even in this short time many houses that had escaped the night before sustained much damage.

'A large tree in the garden of Mr. Tartt, near the College, was snapped off by the wind and falling on the conservatory of Miss Yerbury's house adjoining, did damage to the extent of between £30 and £40. The shop front of Mr. Waite, chemist of Ormond Villas, was also blown in and about 50ft of the high wall between the Royal Hotel yard and Liverpool Place was blown down.

'In the districts around Cheltenham the storm raged with equal fury. Several fine trees in Charlton Park were overturned and the same occurred at Mr. Capel's, Prestbury.'

22 FEBRUARY 1847 Burford Tolsey is a half-timbered building dating from the middle of the sixteenth century, and stands on raised columns with its broad-faced

Burford Tolsey, an attractive façade with stocks, lock-up and whipping-post to the rear.

clock projecting from the gable. In times gone by the Tolsey was the centre of local administration, and taxes were paid here. It was also the courthouse and, justice being swift in former times, law-breakers found guilty were taken there and then to the back of the building to endure either the stocks, the lock-up, or, as recorded on this day in 1847, the whipping-post.

23 FEBRUARY

1846 *Cheltenham Examiner*: 'News arrived in Cheltenham of the Battle of Moodkee between 20,000 British and 60,000 Sikhs. The British, though victorious, lost 149 officers and 3,084 men were killed or wounded. Many of the participants being former residents in Cheltenham, the affair caused great consternation. General Sir Robert Sale, who was killed, resided here before going to India and Lady Sale (since her captivity in Cabul) had been resident in the town and was here when the news of her husband's death arrived. Major F. Somerset, son of Lord and Lady Fitzroy Somerset, was also among the killed.'

24 FEBRUARY

1665 An impressive table tomb in Berkeley churchyard celebrates in rhyme the life of Thomas Pierce, who died at the age of 77. Five times mayor of the town, Pierce was a watchmaker by trade, and the wordsmith who penned his memorial couldn't resist telling us that 'when his own watch was down to the last, he had not key to winde it up'.

25 FEBRUARY

1624 Though long gone, the oldest tombstone in the churchyard of St Mary's, Cheltenham, marked the final resting place of Robert Eckly, who died on this day.

St Mary's Church, Cheltenham.

26 FEBRUARY   **1915**   *Carved on the Great War memorial of the village of Apperley:* 'Sidney Bailey, who lived in Apperley, was mortally wounded when a shell fell into his barracks in Ypres. He was one of five brothers all killed in the war.'

27 FEBRUARY   **1863**   *Cheltenham Examiner:* 'In our obituary today we regret to announce the death of Mrs. Eliza Odella Taylor, widow of the Rev. James Taylor, for so many years incumbent of Clifton, which took place on Thursday last at St. Alban's House, Cheltenham.

'Mrs. Taylor was the daughter of the famous Irish orator, the Right Hon Philpot Curran, Master of the Rolls, and she possessed no small share of her father's wit and humour. It was of her sister (the betrothed of the ill fated Emmet, executed for his share in the abortive insurrection) Moore wrote the touching melody "She is far from the land, where her young hero sleeps".

'The remains of this gifted lady were conveyed from Cheltenham to Clifton yesterday (Tuesday) for interment in the crypt, there to rest "with the smell of mould which nourishes violets".'

28 FEBRUARY   **1987**   The *Stroud News and Journal* on this day referred to the ancient custom of making corn dollies, or corn maidens as they were also known in Gloucester. One design of maiden is called the Nack and in distant days was placed around the neck of any stranger who passed through a village at harvest time. When the stranger moved on, he handed his Nack back to the locals who then cut its head off so that the incomer didn't disappear with the spirit of the corn.

More lively was the custom of young girls making maidens and hiding them under their skirts for young men in the village to try and find.

MARCH

✝

A traditional Gloucestershire saying once heard at this time of year was, 'When you can put your foot on ten daisies, you know Spring is here.' Another served as a weather warning: 'There will be as many frosts in May as there are fogs in March.' Less straightforward perhaps is the once popular local adage, 'A dry March never begs its bread.' Campanologists at the parish church in Cheltenham had to move smartly when in this month in 1343 the tenor bell fell from its beam in the tower and crashed down among them. Remarkably, nobody was injured. But no doubt when the dust had cleared the bell-ringers were reminded that the threat of disaster is always with us. Life can be ticking along nicely, then out of nowhere, disaster strikes. In the chapter that follows we'll see that it can do so in a completely arbitrary way. It can arrive when you're dancing a quadrille, when you're signing a document, or when you're sitting in your front room having a cup of tea and an aeroplane lands on your house.

1 MARCH **1963** Mrs Florence Drury, 85 years old, and two companions were sitting at home in Tuffley Avenue, Gloucester, when an aeroplane landed on the roof. Witnesses watched open-mouthed as the stricken Vickers Varsity stuttered towards its spectacular end, one engine dead and the other failing.

Tragedy in Tuffley Lane, Gloucester.

The enquiry that followed revealed that the pilot, struggling at the controls, was aiming to land the doomed plane in the school playing-fields off Calton Road, but overshot. Both pilot and co-pilot died in the accident, but remarkably Florence Drury and her friends in the house were unscathed.

2 MARCH **1855** *Death of Czar Nicholas I* (a year after the Crimean war between Russia and Britain began). 'A telegram received in Cheltenham, announcing the sudden death of the Emperor of Russia caused immense excitement,' enthused the *Cheltenham Examiner*. 'The Rev. A. Boyd, at Christ Church, said he regarded the event as a distinct answer to prayer. "Only a fortnight ago the people had assembled in the house of God and bowed themselves before him in humble supplication. But none of us could have dreamed in what way our prayers would be answered. None of us could have dreamed that ere ten days had passed, the Angel of Death would come and lay his icy hand on the proud Nicholas and lay him in the dust." Warming to his theme, the Rev. Boyd continued, "Maybe the very commencement of that man's illness would

date from the very day when we knelt in prayer to God. It may be, on that day, the decree went forth, commanding the Angel of Destruction to do his deadly work. In other words, God may have taken this way to make his people understand that the race is not to the swift, nor the battle to the strong; and that his arm is not short, or his ear heavy, but that he listens to, and answers, prayer the same now as he did 1800 years ago."'

1549 William Richmond and Alice Faye of Hempsted found themselves in court charged with cohabiting. Their sentence was to spend the night on their hands and knees praying, while wearing hair shirts. Then, by order of the bishop, they were stripped naked, strapped to a cart and paraded about the village on a Saturday for all to see and mock.

3 MARCH

Canoodlers were forced to parade naked round Hempsted.

1143 *Henry II was born.* Henry ensconced his mistress Rosamund, who came from Frampton-on-Severn, in a house at the middle of a maze so convoluted that only he and his closest knights could reach her. However, Henry's wife, Queen Eleanor of Aquitaine, found her way to the heart of the problem by following a silken thread as it unravelled from her husband's cloak. Eleanor confronted Rosamund with a fatal ultimatum: to die either by dagger or poison. Rosamund chose the latter.

4 MARCH

5 MARCH   **1847**   Cheltenham newspapers reported that 'J. Peart Esq., a gentleman well known and a member of the Board of Commissioners, died suddenly at a board meeting this day. Deceased was in the act of affixing his signature to some official document, when he suddenly laid down his pen, fell back in his chair and instantly expired.'

6 MARCH   **1941**   Staverton was used by the Rotol Flight Test Dept, Folland Aircraft Ltd, GAC Flight Test Dept and other organisations during the Second World War to test aeronautical developments. The airfield was also a training centre. With so much experimental work and so many inexperienced flyers centred on Staverton, it is hardly surprising that accidents and incidents were far from infrequent.

One wartime story recalls that a young pilot crashed his Tiger Moth to the rear of the Plough Inn on the old A40. Struggling from the wreckage, he staggered into the pub to order a stiff drink and was told by the landlord he would have to wait his turn to be served, just like all the other crashed pilots who used the bar.

7 MARCH   **1947**   Before prevention work was carried out in the 1950s, flooding in Gloucester's Westgate Street and the surrounding lanes was an annual event. The worst occasion was in this year, when the Severn rose 15ft 4in above its normal level and virtually everywhere west of the Cross was inundated. Many houses towards the lower end of Westgate were flooded up to the first storey

Flooding was a regular misery in Westgate.

and families had to be rescued by Red Cross boats. The nave of St Nicholas's church was under water, as was the A40 out of the city as far as Over. Then in 1947 came the Big Freeze, followed by the Big Flood.

Early in that year extraordinarily heavy rainfall was followed by bitterly cold weather. At the end of February temperatures of −25°F were recorded, which meant that vast volumes of water were locked into ice, waiting to be released.

The thaw began on 7 March and the Severn rose rapidly. Soon hundreds had to abandon their homes as floodwaters surged up Westgate Street to lap at the steps of Shire Hall. Temporary accommodation was found in church halls, and the council provided over 20,000 hot meals to the homeless. St Nicholas's Church was awash, which added a touch of irony to the chaos. St Nicholas is the patron saint of sailors.

1849 'Col John Wolridge, of Cleveland House [Cheltenham], destroyed himself by jumping into the Marle Hill pond. The deceased, who was in his 69th year, had been in an unsettled state of mind for some time from the effects of a railway accident.'

8 MARCH

1904 Sydney George Smith had the dubious distinction of being the only Cheltonian ever to be hanged in Gloucester gaol. Smith lived in the town with Alice Woodman, in abject poverty. Their few possessions sold or pawned, Smith decided to bring an end to the misery he and Alice shared. He cut her throat as she slept, then turned the razor on himself. Neighbours discovered him, severely wounded but alive, and called for help. The unfortunate man was restored to health, found guilty of murder and hanged. Unlike all previous executions at the county gaol, Smith's hanging was not preceded by a notice pinned to the prison gate. The gaol bell was not tolled and no black flag was hoisted after his dispatch.

9 MARCH

1919 Arthur Inglis holds a unique place in the history of tank warfare. A pupil of Cheltenham College, he joined the Glosters when hostilities began in 1914. The First World War was riddled with absurdities, one of which was that when tanks went into action they were preceded by a commanding officer on foot.

10 MARCH

Major Arthur Inglis was the first man in history to lead tanks into action. He did so in 1916 at the Battle of Flers Courcelles in the Somme sector. Remarkably, Inglis survived this honour/ordeal, but was injured in 1918 and died in March the following year from his wounds. He is buried in Prestbury churchyard.

First World War tanks were led into battle by an officer on foot. This photograph was taken at Westal Green, Cheltenham, in about 1920.

11 MARCH **1937** In the 1930s Arthur Bullock and his brother-in-law Bert looked after Gloucester people from head to toe. Arthur had a barber shop in Worcester Street, while Bert was a cobbler in Alvin Street.

In 1932 Arthur's second son Jack contracted tuberculosis and was taken to Over isolation hospital. On a visit, Arthur learned that no barber would visit the hospital for fear of catching the disease. The matron asked Albert if he would take on the task, assuring him that if he took a laxative after each visit he wouldn't catch TB.

Arthur took the job and the laxatives, but in time became infected. By 1936 he was too ill to continue his business, so he sold the barber shop and was admitted to Over as a patient.

In the meantime, Bert had fallen sick too and was forced to give up his cobbling hammers. Bert was taken into hospital and put in the bed adjacent to his brother-in-law. Both men died on the same day, and were given a double funeral at St John's church, Northgate Street in March 1937, on Arthur's thirtieth wedding anniversary.

12 MARCH **1905** *Hero Henry Hook VC died.* This Churcham agricultural labourer won the highest award for bravery in the Battle of Rorke's Drift. Hook was a hospital cook who had the misfortune to find himself one of 1,000 British soldiers facing a hostile army of 4,500 Zulus. When the battle began, Hook was in the hospital hut. Isolated from the rest of his countrymen, he had to defend a dozen patients against continuous onslaught. Despite a wound to the head, Hook saved those in his care and returned home a hero.

On retirement from the army, Hook worked for twenty-three years as a doorman at the British Museum. Then suffering ill health, he returned to Gloucester and lived at 2 Osborn Villas, Roseberry Avenue. When he died at the age of 55, thousands of local people lined the route from Gloucester to Churcham, where Henry Hook is buried.

13 MARCH **1847** It was reported on this day that 'A young lady, Miss Julia Quinlan, died suddenly while dancing a quadrille at a ball given by Lieut Col Fitzmaurice, at his residence in Berkeley.'

14 MARCH **1950** During this month a Churchdown-based amateur dramatic group called the Unknown Players travelled to Mountain Ash in South Wales to stage a play entitled *The Sacred Flame*. After the performance they returned home to learn that their headquarters, Sandycroft Social Club, had burned to the ground.

1933 Bertram Mills' Circus set up its big top at the athletic ground (now a housing estate) in Albion Street, Cheltenham. The thrills, spills and entertainment included 'Lineret – the human cannon ball', and the crowd held its breath in eager anticipation as the slim figure slipped into the muzzle of the impressive artillery piece. A flash! A bang! And Lineret was seen to shoot out of the barrel, landing a good distance off in the safety net. Three weeks later, when performing in Bath, the safety net was not so well positioned and Lineret was killed.

15 MARCH

1932 This was a busy month for Gloucester's fire brigade. The first major conflagration was at the *Gloucester Citizen* premises. Fire broke out in the basement and progressed upwards via the lift shaft. It took firemen two hours to bring the blaze under control, by which time the St John's Lane building was gutted.

16 MARCH

The next fire was at Priestley's Studios Ltd in Commercial Road. Fire was discovered at the photographic business at 5 a.m. on a Saturday morning, and once more the local brigade had a hard fight on its hands.

Just two days later W.C. Matthews' furniture store in Barton Street blazed. Fire-retardant materials were, of course, a distant development in 1932, and within ten minutes the showroom was a raging bonfire of fast-burning chairs, sofas, tables and carpets.

It was all hands to the pump for Gloucester Fire Brigade on this day in 1932.

17 MARCH

A happy event at Hayden Green. Seven children and 14s a week to live on!

1908 Mr and Mrs Ball were thrice blessed when on St Patrick's Day their triplets, two boys and a girl, entered the world. Mrs Ball was photographed with the babies at their home in Hayden Green, which, as the *Gloucestershire Graphic* minced no words describing, was 'just at the entrance to the corporation sewerage farm'.

The trio of newborns brought the Balls' tally of offspring to seven. Life couldn't have been easy. 'The husband's wages as a farm labourer amount to only 14 shillings per week and he has to work from four o'clock in the morning to six o'clock at night. Out of this has to be provided food and clothes for the family of nine, besides rent for the cottage.' So much for the good old days.

CHELTENHAM CHRONICLE AND GLOUCESTERSHIRE GRAPHIC

TRIPLETS NEAR CHELTENHAM
On St. Patrick's Day, March 17th, 1908, Mrs. Ball, wife of Mr. W. H. Ball, a farm labourer, of Hayden Green, near Cheltenham, presented her husband with triplets two boys and a girl

18 MARCH

1912 Despite a superhuman struggle in appalling weather conditions, the British expedition led by Captain Robert Falcon Scott, and including Edward Wilson of Cheltenham, arrived at the South Pole on 18 January 1912 to find the Norwegian flag already planted in the icy wasteland. The party, led by Amundsen, had beaten them to the prize by thirty-three days.

Their energy expended by the useless dash for glory, probably less well quipped than they should have been, and weakened by disappointment, Scott's explorers began the long trek back towards their base at Cape Evans. If anything the weather was worse on the return. Food and fuel supplies ran low, illness and frostbite took their toll. Then, to add to the misery, Petty Officer Evans took a fall on the Beardmore Glacier and died soon after of concussion.

Oates was the next fatality. Crippled and sick, but not wishing to spoil what chance there might be of his fellows reaching safety, Oates delivered the immortal words 'I am just going outside and may be some time', and was never seen again.

Scott, Wilson and Bowers were the last to survive, though they knew what their fate was to be, as the final entry in the leader's diary reveals. 'I do not think we can hope for better things now. We shall stick it out to the end, but we are getting weaker, of course, and the end cannot be far. It seems a pity, but I do not think I can write more.'

The three died huddled together in March 1912. They were just 11 miles from a food depot. In November of that year their bodies and Scott's diaries were found in the small, snow-covered tent.

The memorial to Antarctic hero Edward Wilson was unveiled in Cheltenham Promenade.

1858   An eclipse of the sun was followed by a violent storm, which dealt residents of a cottage in Arle a severe blow: 'lightning struck the roof and passed from room to room in the most strange manner. A chimney was knocked off, a window and frame carried bodily into the room, the doors of a wardrobe cut open, as from the blow of a hatchet, the flooring was in several places torn up, and solid masses of brickwork and masonry were cracked and splintered.'

19 MARCH

1946   Until the 1960s Gloucester's cattle market stood in the centre of the city, and market days could be unusually lively. On this day a farmer from Andoversford brought a cow and her young calf. When the two were separated, the mother went wild and ran amok. First the animal knocked over a pram in which a baby was asleep. Then the desperate creature dashed out of market square (now the bus station), tossed a Mr Bridgeman, who had just emerged from the Co-op, high into the air and ran down Brunswick Road. Eventually the animal was cornered in St Michael's Square and was about to be put down when a thoughtful soul had the idea of reuniting the mother with its offspring. The calf was brought, the cow calmed down and all was well. Except of course for the unfortunate Mr Bridgeman.

20 MARCH

1955   A similar event took place at Gloucester's cattle market when a bull escaped and ran willy-nilly about the city centre. All attempts at capture failed, but the hefty problem resolved itself when the bull caught a glimpse of itself reflected in the window of a café. At full pelt, he charged, smashed straight through the front of the building and was knocked out stone cold when he collided with the back wall.

21 MARCH

21 MARCH 1801 Alone among the regiments of the British Army, the Glosters – now amalgamated into the Royal Glo'shire, Berkshire and Wiltshire Regiment – wear the famous back badge on their head gear. This tradition dates back to the Battle of Alexandria, which took place this year. At that time Napoleon's armies reigned supreme in Europe, although his ambitions ranged further. With a jealous eye on Britain's empire in India, the French general invaded Egypt, meaning to take control of this essential communications link between Europe and the Far East.

Under the leadership of Sir Ralph Abercrombie, the British army forced a hotly contested landing at Aboukir Bay and advanced towards the French stronghold of Alexandria. After an inconclusive clash between British and French, Abercrombie's forces held defensive positions some three miles from the town.

The 28th Glosters were posted on a low ridge, where they established a redoubt not far from an ancient Roman fort. Under cover of darkness the French made a surprise attack, employing their crack Invincible Legion to engage the Glosters on their front, while simultaneously sweeping by on both flanks. This succeeded in cutting off the local regiment and a fierce, hand-to-hand struggle began. When daylight came, the Glosters found themselves in an even more perilous position when French cavalry was brought against them. Time and again the Glosters came under attack, but despite depleted numbers and their unsupported position, they managed to hold. Then a second body of French cavalry was brought into the affray with the order to assault the

The battle of Alexandria.
Below: The Glosters won the back badge at this battle.

Glosters from the rear. Under this extreme pressure, the Glosters were ordered 'Rear rank 28th, right about face', and the regiment stood back-to-back firing volleys at the oncoming French.

For another four hours the battle raged, by which time the Glosters were so short of ammunition that some of their number could do no more than throw rocks. But by sheer tenacity they wore down their attackers, and the French retreated. The Glosters paid a high price in lives lost, including that of General Abercrombie. But the victory was crucial, because if Napoleon had succeeded in ousting the British presence in Egypt, the way would have been open for another power, France, Russia, or Japan, to take control of India. History would have been very different.

Two centuries on, the date on which the Battle of Alexandria was fought, 21 March, is still celebrated by the Glosters as Back Badge Day.

23 MARCH 1827 'Every species of profligacy – adultery, fornication, uncleanliness, lasciviousness, hatred, violence, emulations, wrath, strife, envying, drunkenness, revellings and such like are promoted by race week. If you wish your child to plunge into the world's vain pleasures, to acquire the taste for dissipation, send him to Cheltenham races.' *Dean Francis Close.*

1643 *The Battle of Highnam*. Besides being a bloody business, this was the last time that Welsh and English took up arms against one another. The event preceded the siege of Gloucester. An army of 2,600 Welshmen under the command of Sir Jerome Brett was entrenched at Highnam awaiting the arrival of Prince Rupert, with whose help they proposed to take the city.

After five weeks waiting, the Welsh learned that Prince Rupert had decided not to come. But by this time Colonel Massey, commander of Gloucester, had sent word to General Waller, his Parliamentarian ally in Wiltshire. Waller's reputation as an efficient, merciless military man was well justified. Under cover of darkness and bolstered by 500 men from the city, Waller's army surrounded the Welsh. Taken by surprise, outnumbered and out-positioned, the Welsh were routed, and 600 of them were killed, the rest taken prisoner in St Mary de Lode Church.

In 1886 workmen in Highnam uncovered a battle grave containing the bones of eighty-six soldiers who fell. These were buried at Barbers Bridge beneath a cross built from the stones of the old city wall.

24 MARCH

1855 Stephen Curtis, while building a vault in the churchyard of Charlton Kings, was buried beneath the soil, and, when he was dug out, was found to be quite dead.

25 MARCH

1941 At 4 o'clock in the afternoon this day shoppers in Gloucester were stopped in their tracks by the sight of a Luftwaffe Ju88 flying at little more than rooftop height over the city centre. It was followed a few seconds later by an RAF Hurricane in hot pursuit. So unexpected was the spectacle that nobody bothered to take cover. They watched as though hypnotised as four bombs dropped from the twin-engined Ju88 to land in the Barton Street area.

Six people were killed and twenty-seven more injured in the attack, which resulted in a church and eighteen houses being flattened. In Millbrook Street chapel a mothers' meeting was in progress when the building was hit and wrecked, but amazingly nobody was hurt.

Such was the violence of the blast that a section of railway line was lifted from near Eastgate Street station (where Asda is now) and deposited in a Denmark Road garden.

26 MARCH

1908 When the Great Western Railway constructed Malvern Road station in Cheltenham, with its curving main platform 700ft in length, to serve the new Honeybourne line, hundreds of townspeople had to be rehoused. The development meant demolishing seventy dwellings in Great Western Road, Bloomsbury Place, Carlton Place, Hill View Cottages, Marsh Cottages and Whitehall Street. A pub named the Cherry Tree was knocked down too. The new line also cut through the old town cemetery, and 300 bodies had to be removed to another resting place.

27 MARCH

Malvern Road station. The new line cut through old town cemetery.

28 MARCH   **1846**   *Cheltenham Examiner*: 'News arrived of the Battle of Aliwal, when 12,000 British troops under Sir Harry Smith defeated the Sikhs, 24,000 strong, and captured 65 guns. Our loss was 600 in killed and wounded. Among the Cheltenham officers who fell in this engagement were Lieutenant Smallpage and Captain Knowles, nephew of Colonel Austin, of Lansdown Place.

'At the annual meeting of the Naval and Military Bible Society, a few days after the news of these losses arrived, the Rev. F. Close observed "I do say as a Christian minister, I do firmly believe in the lawfulness of war under the present circumstance of the world and under the restrictions and influences of Christianity; and I do think that those who owe their independence, their prosperity, their easy arm chair and all the blessing of home to the gallantry – under God – to the gallantry and devotion of British seamen and soldiers, ought not to prattle so much about the unlawfulness of war, for had it not been for men of other determinations and dispositions, they would have been in a very different position themselves." He continued in this vein for some while.'

29 MARCH   **1750**   John Stafford Smith of Gloucester was christened in the cathedral on this day. He composed the tune to the 'Stars and Stripes', which was some time later adopted by the United States of America as its national anthem, died in 1836 when a grape pip became lodged in his throat.

30 MARCH   **1891**   *Cheltenham Examiner*: 'Melee reported at Cheltenham College. The man who was privileged to sell pancakes to the students on Shrove Tuesday not giving satisfaction in the quality of his edibles, a number of his customers invaded his stall and amused themselves for some time by pelting the vendor with his own pancakes. The affair was at one time likely to be brought before the magistrates but was ultimately arranged out of court.'

31 MARCH   **1858**   Much excitement was caused in Cheltenham by a report that the emperor of the French had been assassinated. It appeared that a telegram was received giving the result of the University boat race, in which was the passage 'the *Emperor* shot ahead'. By some mistake the words were read, and the news disseminated, as 'the Emperor shot dead'.

April

✠

In the eighteenth century John Nelson was the landlord of the New Inn, Northgate Street, Gloucester. He staged regular events at the hostelry, some of a bizarre nature. The New Inn's reputation for freak shows was established in 1749 when a mermaid captured off the coast of Mexico was exhibited at the pub for two weeks. In April 1761 a waxworks exhibition of the newly crowned monarch George III, and other members of the royal family, drew large crowds. The likenesses were the work of a Mr Salmon who hailed from Fleet Street, London. Entry to the show, open from 10 a.m. until 10 p.m., was 6d, or 3d for children and servants. In 1770 Maria Theresa, billed as the 'Corsican Fairy', appeared at the inn. This minuscule maiden was 27 years old, weighed 26lb and stood 2ft 10in tall.

1 APRIL   **1939**   Statistics about executions in Gloucester gaol make grim, but revealing reading. Between 1786 and 1939, 140 prisoners were executed – 132 men and 8 women. April was the month when most hangings took place (67), followed by August (30) and March (13). The only month in which nobody was ever executed was October.

The majority (42) were hanged for murder. (From 1879 this was the only crime for which executions took place locally.) The second largest group (22) were hanged for burglary. Third on the list came horse and sheep stealing, both crimes for which 17 convicts were executed. Two were hanged for stealing wheat, two for arson, two for unspecified theft and two for rape. Eight men were despatched for robbery, another eight for housebreaking, and seven for shooting people. In 1814 a man was hanged for forgery, and in 1800 Joseph Stevens of Minchinhampton was sentenced to death for 'cutting cloth from racks'. The youngest man hanged was 16, the oldest 70. The youngest woman hanged was 21 and the oldest 69. Most (94) were aged between 20 and 30.

Patrick Dalton, hanged in 1817, came from Sligo in Ireland, giving him the dubious privilege of having come further than anyone else to be executed in the city.

Three Cheltenham men were hanged in 1872, 1886 and 1904, all for murder, as was a single Tewkesburian in 1791. Two Gloucestrians were hanged: Joss Richards in 1818 for robbery and John Sparrow in 1826 for sheep stealing.

2 APRIL   **1875**   In years gone by a foot ferry crossed the Avon from Twyning Fleet to the Bredon side of the river. On this day a two-horse dray laden with casks of beer was being carried across when the animals panicked and tipped the boat over. The ferryman swam safely to the bank, heroically saving the drayman as well, but the two horses drowned.

3 APRIL   **1990**   Earth tremors were felt in northern parts of the county on this day. Those with long memories may recall the more serious seismological disturbance of 1926, which was said to cause the appearance of cracks in the Devil's Chimney at Leckhampton (opposite). But these events pale to insignificance when compared to the earthquake that hit Cheltenham in the fourteenth century, when serious damage was done to St Mary's parish church and 600 local inhabitants were rendered homeless.

4 APRIL   **1942**   This day was Easter Saturday. At the Gloster Aircraft Company's factory in Hucclecote the day shift was leaving at about 4.30 p.m. when two Luftwaffe raiders appeared, low in the sky. Six bombs fell. One landed on a bus waiting to take workers home from GAC's crowded car park. The works' number-one canteen and number-eight workshop were destroyed, and there was a further blast in the machine shop. A block-house was wrecked, and it took four hours to bring under control the fires that raged around the devastated area.

The Devil's Chimney at
Leckhampton: earthquake was
a cracker in 1926.

At 5.25 on the same afternoon a second raid took place, followed by a third at 6.10 p.m. A house opposite the factory took a direct hit and all five occupants were killed, including an eleven-month-old baby. Two more houses to the east of the airfield were also damaged.

Official figures tell us that ten men, five women and three children died in these Easter raids, with some two hundred people injured.

5 APRIL **1965** Elvers were once a nutritious, seasonal feed for working people who lived along the banks of the Severn. If you caught them yourself they had the distinct advantage of being free. Even so, elvers were never a meal for the faint-hearted, and Susan Severn, writing in the *Gloucester Journal*, was plainly not a fan. She wrote, 'Even the most ardent elver enthusiast couldn't faithfully say they look very lovely. To look in your frying pan and see your dinner squirming about with what appears like thick saliva cannot be very appetising. And a mass of white worms on a plate might not be everyone's idea of gastronomic bliss.'

6 APRIL **1949** Steel shortages meant that new cars were difficult to come by in post-Second World War Britain. The enterprising Mr C.D. Waters of Southam decided to overcome the problem by designing and building his own. What began as a hobby turned into an obsession, and Mr Waters devoted some 3,500 hours to the making of his CDW prototype, which was registered HAD 1.

All the hard work paid off though, because the end result was a sleek, open-topped sportster capable of well over 100mph and a fairly frugal 32mpg. News of the CDW reached Jaguar, and the Coventry-based motor-maker showed interest in putting Mr Waters' design into production, which of course looked certain to make him a very wealthy man indeed. A meeting was arranged for the people from Jaguar to visit Southam and take a look at the CDW. The day before they were due to arrive, on the Easter weekend, the barn adjacent to Mr Waters' garage caught fire and his car was destroyed.

7 APRIL **1889** A Forest of Dean story tells how an Italian roamer arrived in Ruardean leading a bear. When a crowd gathered around the curious couple, the man began to play a violin, which prompted his tethered companion to stand upright and shuffle a laborious jig. Local people were no doubt engaged by the spectacle. Entertainment of any kind was a rarity, and soon coins of appreciation clinked into the violinist's hat providing enough money for the pair to put up at the local inn.

Next morning a grisly sight met the two village boys who sneaked into the pub stables where the bear had been penned for the night. In the straw was the body of a local girl, mauled and gored. Once the alarm had been raised, the villagers bayed for revenge. A group armed with cudgels burst in on the bear and beat the creature to death. They then turned their attentions to the Italian owner, who fled for his life.

Some months later it emerged that the girl had fallen victim not to the bear, but to a village man who had assaulted and murdered her before dumping the body in the bear's pen to place the blame on the unfortunate bruno.

A bear under suspicion of killing a young girl was brutally beaten to death at Ruardean.

1792   For centuries, executions in Gloucester were carried out on waste ground near Over bridge. But when the new county gaol opened, the flat roof of its entrance lodge became the venue for hangings. The first execution took place this month, when Charles Rackford was despatched for highway robbery.

8 APRIL

In 1811 William Townley was hanged in Gloucester, even though he had been granted a reprieve. The stay of execution was sent to the Sheriff of Gloucester from Hereford the evening before Townley was scheduled to meet his maker. Unfortunately, the reprieve was wrongly addressed and so arrived 20 minutes too late.

1862   *Cheltenham Examiner*: 'Terrible accident at Thackwell's brickyard. A man named Charles Luker got his arm in the machine and attracted by his screams another man named Colley rushed to the spot and in his endeavours to save his companion had the fingers of one hand crushed and the fingers of the other cut off and dragged completely from one hand. Mrs. Thackwell, who happened to be near, with great presence of mind applied the brake and so no doubt saved the fellows from still more serious injuries.'

9 APRIL

10 APRIL 1818 'William Lake, a native of Boddington, died there in his 99th year. He was in the constant and daily habit of walking to Cheltenham and back again – a distance both ways of nine miles – until a few days previous to his death and to the last he perfectly possessed his mental faculties'. (*Norman's History of Cheltenham*, John Goding, published 1863).

11 APRIL 1722 The first issue of the *Gloucester Journal*, published by Robert Raikes from an office in Northgate Street, appeared this month. His son, also named Robert, who was the pioneer of Sunday schools, died in 1811. At his funeral were numerous children who had benefited from the education they had received at the city Sunday schools he was instrumental in establishing. In accordance with Raikes' wishes, each of the young mourners received one shilling and a plum pudding.

12 APRIL 1803 An epitaph in St Mary's parish church, Cheltenham, is said to be the longest in the country. It tells the story of how Henry Skillicorne, a retired sea captain who died this day, discovered the spa that resulted in Cheltenham's rise to fame and fashionable fortune in the eighteenth century. 'He was an excellent sea man of tryed courage', reads the plaque, 'and could do business in seven tongues. He was so temperate as never to have been once intoxicated. Religious without hypocrisy, grave without austerity, of a cheerful conversation without levity, a kind husband and tender father.' The eulogy goes on in a similar vein for paragraph after paragraph.

13 APRIL 1865 In the garden of Fish Cottage at Blockley, near Chipping Campden, is the grave of a pet trout, which died at the age of twenty years this month in 1865. The fish was owned by a Mr Keyte, whose son Charles composed the rhyme found on the headstone.

> Under the soil the old fish do lie.
> 20 years he lived and then did die.
> He was so tame you understand
> He would come and eat out of your hand.

14 APRIL 1836 Harriet Tarver was hanged at Gloucester for poisoning her husband. A ballad describing how she had been driven to commit the crime was produced by Thomas Willey, a Cheltenham rhymester, who had his own printing press in the High Street.

15 APRIL 1843 From the *Bath & Cheltenham Gazette*. 'A mischievous young urchin named Henry Mitchell was summoned before the magistrates of Cheltenham on Thursday se'night [week] for causing an obstruction on the Birmingham and Gloucester railway at Badgeworth. It appears that he stood on the bridge and scattered ashes on the line for the purpose of throwing the engine off the rails. Fortunately it was discovered in time and the boy was sent to Northleach [house of correction] for two months.'

From elsewhere in the same newspaper: 'There has been another sad instance of the melancholy effects of the prison discipline of Northleach. A young man of the town, by the name of Jones, who had originally been committed for petty larceny, was discharged from prison, but in so weak and emaciated a state, it is said from the wheel [treadmill] and prison diet, that he was utterly unable to walk, and was taken home in a fly, although when he went to prison he was a strong, healthy lad. For three weeks he lingered on in a miserable state, but it appears that his constitution had been so reduced that medical aid became of no avail and he expired last Wednesday. A more miserable exhibition of absolute starvation we never beheld. On enquiry we were told that the toil at the Northleach wheel was so severe, and the cravings of hunger so intolerable, that he has at times kicked the dogs away from their bones in order that he himself might gnaw them.'

16 APRIL **1964**   Until the closure of the line in this year, if you travelled on the train from Tetbury to Kemble you could instruct the driver to stop at Trouble House Halt. One of the least well-appointed railway destinations in the land, this had no platform. Instead passengers stepped down from the carriage onto a beer crate provided by the nearby Trouble House pub.

If ever a hostelry was appropriately named, this is the one. During the English Civil War a bloody skirmish took place here when Royalists out for an ale or two were surprised by a group of Roundheads. In 1829 brothers Mathias and Henry Finnel, two notorious highwaymen of the time, put up lively resistance before being overpowered at the pub and summarily hanged.

Soon afterwards a gang of Luddites who popped in for a drink, after a rampage of arson attacks on farm buildings and machinery in the locality, found themselves surrounded by troops sent to apprehend them. A bloody brawl ensued before the Luddites were arrested and removed to Dursley gaol.

Later in the century the debt-laden landlord hanged himself from a beam, and was succeeded by a host who promptly committed suicide by drowning himself in a pond close by.

At one time the pub was called the Wagon and Horses. You can understand why the name was changed.

17 APRIL **1740**   An epitaph in Holy Trinity Church, Badgeworth, is notable for its florid style and random use of capital letters.

> Reader – Let this Marble be a Monitor to the
> Living as well as a Memorial of the
> Dead, and, when thou readest the name of
> Littleton Lawrence Esq
> be instructed not to place thy Confidence
> in the most Corporeal Excellences,
> which, like his, must undergo the deformity of Corruption.
> And let his Virtues excite thy Imagination, particularly his parental
> Affection, Inflexible Honesty, and Christian
> Benevolence, which, through a steadfast Faith
> in the Redeemer, will advance thee to a Life
> immortal and full of Glory.

He died this month aged 54.

18 APRIL **1844**   *Cheltenham Examiner*: 'A son of Lady Russell, of Montpellier House, shot by accidental discharge of a fowling piece at Charlton Park. The bone of the leg was so much shattered as to render amputation of the limb absolutely necessary to save the patient's life.'

19 APRIL **1860**   An announcement described the 'Distressing accident to Mr. Hanks, Manor Farm, Charlton Abbots. Mr. Hanks, his son Thomas, and the Messrs. Beckinsale of this town were going out for an hour's rabbit shooting, when the gun of one of the last named gentlemen was accidentally discharged and the content entering the head and neck of Mr. Hanks junior, aged 17, caused his instant death.'

1836 *Gloucester's miser-millionaire Jemmy Wood died.* The proprietor of a local bank, Wood watched every penny very closely, and never contributed to charity. He dressed in rags, rarely washed and scrounged lumps of coal in the docks for a little free warmth in winter. Rather than pay the price of a ride, he once hitched a lift from Tewkesbury to Gloucester lying flat out in the back of a hearse. He left £781,000, a vast sum in today's values.

20 APRIL

1933 Nesta Lane (aka Lewis and Nesta of the Forest) was one of the last people in the country to be brought to court under the Witchcraft Act of 1735. She appeared before magistrates in Gloucester in sylvan green tunic and nun-like headdress, carrying a crucifix in one hand and a framed icon in the other.

21 APRIL

That old black magic reported in the *Citizen*.

Nesta, a self-proclaimed clairvoyante, medium, prophet and healer, gave consultations in a hired room above the Pilgrims' Rest café in Worcester Street, Gloucester. She was summoned to appear in court by the city authorities following undercover investigations by the Gloucestershire Constabulary, and was charged on two counts of 'fortune telling to deceive and impose on His Majesty's subjects'.

She denied both charges, but was found guilty under the Witchcraft Act and fined £2 8s. This she refused to pay until threatened with a two-week spell in prison. The Witchcraft Act, incidentally, was repealed in 1951.

In the 1960s Nesta cropped up again, this time in the national newspapers, when she was living in St Margaret's Road, Cheltenham. A couple employed by Nesta to do odd jobs were accused by her of stealing a garden spade. When they failed to return it, she cast a spell on them by writing 'They who steal a spade shall dig a grave for the one they know best' on three separate sheets of paper. One copy of the spell was posted to the couple, another buried in Nesta's garden and the third burned. Within a short space of time the couple's baby and the wife's mother died.

22 April   **1951**   The Glosters found themselves in the front line at the crucial battle of Imjin River, Korea, on this day. Taking part in the action was Platoon Commander Denys Whatmore of Cheltenham, a national service volunteer.

Local regiment the Glosters were in the front line.

This description is taken from his book *One Road to Imjin*: 'The dawn came and we were so engaged in the fight that it was full daylight before we knew it. At about 0530 hours, the Chinese over-ran part of No. 1 section, got into the slit trenches there and opened fire on the rest of us. I had a glimpse of a young Chinese in a steel helmet, mouth open, shouting, and then he threw a grenade at me. It flew towards my trench, the wooden handle gyrating in the air, and I just had time to yell 'Grenade' to warn the others, and to duck, when it fell on the breastwork of the lip of the trench. It teetered, dropped back outside the breastwork and exploded with an awful bang, showering us with stones.'

Perched on Hill 235 overlooking the Imjin River, the Glosters held back the advance of the Chinese 63rd army for several days. By the third night of the battle they were completely surrounded, but continued to fight to the last bullet. The survivors spent the rest of the war in North Korean prisoner of war camps.

1858   'Accounts received of the death of Lieutenant Power, late a pupil of Cheltenham College, at a tiger hunt in India. Power attacked a huge tiger with great gallantry, but, his attendants running away, the brute seized the poor fellow and shook him like a dog worrying vermin. When assistance arrived Lt Power was only able to exclaim 'I am dying' and instantly expired.' (*Norman's History of Cheltenham*, John Goding, published 1863).

23 APRIL

A former Cheltenham College pupil was killed by a tiger.

24 APRIL 1908   The *Gloucestershire Graphic* reported that a white bull belonging to farmer George Hannis of Churchdown 'was born with only three legs, there being no semblance of a leg where the fourth should have been; the three are in their natural positions. The calf has done remarkably well, but looks most ludicrous when galloping about in play.'

25 APRIL 1597   The Mickleton Hooter is said to be the ghost of Sir Edward Greville's only son and heir, who was shot by his landowning father when mistaken for a robber at a spot called Weeping Hollow. Stricken with grief, Sir Edward sold up and left forever.

Sleepy Mickleton is haunted by Hooter.

26 APRIL 1862   A sports day at a local school was marred by an unfortunate incident reported this day. 'At the College athletic sports a serious accident occurred to one of the pupils, Mr. Laurence Garnett. He was vaulting with the pole and had already topped a height of 7'11' when, on the next rise, his pole broke short off, and, falling on his back, he sustained so severe an injury to the spine that for some while his life was despaired of.'

27 APRIL 1766   The *Gentleman's Magazine* included information concerning the death of a young reveller named Richard Parsons. At a card session in Chalford,

Parsons became so convinced that he was being taken for a ride that he leapt to his feet and declared, 'May I never enter the kingdom of Heaven and may my flesh rot on my bones if I am not being cheated at this table.'

Shortly afterwards Parsons became the victim of an undiagnosed disease, which began with his leg becoming mortified. The malady spread quickly and the unfortunate Parsons passed away in agony so great that the undertaker was unable to close the eyes of his corpse.

A doctor named Peglar from Minchinhampton was present when the body was laid out, and wrote that it was curiously rotted and discoloured, giving the appearance of having been in the grave for about six months.

28 APRIL **1856** In the third quarter of the nineteenth century, Prestbury boasted four jockeys – George Stevens, Tom Oliver, William Holman and William Archer – who between them won the Grand National, traditionally run this month, a dozen times. The most celebrated of these was George Stevens, who won the first of five Grand Nationals on this day riding Freetrader. This was followed by others on Emblem in 1861, Emblematic in 1864 and The Colonel in 1869 and 1870.

Stevens was a national sporting star, and after each of his Aintree triumphs the celebrated rider arrived home to find blazing beacons on Cleeve Hill heralding home the hero. Never once in his 20-year career did Stevens sustain serious injury, but he met an unfitting fate when riding to his home on the hill. A sudden gust of wind took his hat off and unsteadied his mount, which stumbled on a drainpipe. The champion jockey was unsaddled, hit the ground and later died. A small stone memorial near the turning to Southam from the old A46 (now the B4632 Winchcombe Road) marks the spot.

Jockey George Stevens – killed when his hat blew off.

29 APRIL **1896** In many Gloucestershire churches we find reminders that old pagan images were incorporated into Christianity. On the outside walls of North Cerney church a brace of sixteenth-century carved figures can be seen – and most odd they are. About 4ft in length, each is the likeness of a manticore. This mythical creature had the head of a man, with three rows of teeth, the body of a lion, and the tail of a scorpion. Manticores were said to feed on a diet of naked people, so the best way to avoid falling prey

Naked people were manticores' favourite snack.

to their attentions was to remain fully clothed at all times. The carvings were uncovered on this day during restoration work.

30 APRIL   **1532**   In the church at Westbury-on-Severn, a chained book can be found – not a Bible as is usually the way with chained books, but a copy of Foxe's *Book of Martyrs*. In it the execution of James Baynham is recorded. The son of the lord of the manor, Baynham is believed to be the only person from the Forest of Dean to be martyred for his beliefs. He was burned at the stake on this day.

MAY

✠

*Peace and quiet were put to one side in Cheltenham on 3 May 1471
when Edward IV passed through the insignificant little market town with
3,000 infantry troops, plus cavalry. They were on their way to Tewkesbury to do
battle with the house of Lancaster, and won. Less well known than the Battle of
Tewkesbury is the Battle of May Hill, which once took place on May Day each
year. On one side were local youths dressed in the garb of winter, while their
opponents wore symbols of spring. The battle was more a rough and tumble than
all-out war and by popular tradition spring always won. The victory was
celebrated by carrying green branches about the locality while singing, 'We have
brought the summer home'. A remnant of the Battle of May Hill is the annual
gathering of Morris men who turn out at dawn, then take the summer on to
Newent. On 28 May 1984 just after coming off stage after a charity show at the
Roses Theatre, Tewkesbury, Eric Morecambe (real name John Eric Bartholomew)
suffered his third and final heart attack. He was taken to Cheltenham General
Hospital, where he died in the early hours of the following morning. He was 58.*

1 MAY   **1876**   On this day the first issue of the *Citizen* appeared on the streets of Gloucester, price one halfpenny. It included a report on the case of James Griffin who was charged with causing a disturbance in the docks, where he had been found 'dancing about' behind the Mariner's Chapel by Constable Murray. Griffin replied to the policeman's request that he move on by punching him in the face.

Speaking on behalf of the prisoner, the Revd Jo Turner 'believed him to be insane and a source of some danger to the public. This was attributed to the prisoner being in the army for ten years, during which time he suffered sunstroke.' The good reverend suggested that this experience, when blended with even the smallest amount of intoxicating liquor, caused insanity. Griffin was held on remand.

1930 Scandal rocked Churchdown when a resident of the village, Arthur Harris, appeared at the Old Bailey charged with double bigamy. The 34-year-old, who gave his address as The Gables, Churchdown, Gloucestershire, pleaded not guilty.

The story unfolded that during the First World War Harris had been a 2nd lieutenant in the Royal Flying Corps. Then came a long catalogue of affairs and bigamous marriages, mostly to women he met in Hyde Park. When two or three of the wives somehow learned that they were married to the same man, they confronted their shared lothario. Very tranquil types the wronged women must have been, because they pronounced that if Harris left the country, no more would be said about his multiple indiscretions.

Probably gratefully, Harris caught the next ship to New Zealand. Arriving down under, he found digs and, soon back into his stride, arranged to marry his landlady, but was picked up by the police before wedding bells sounded once again. Sentencing Harris to five years, the Common Sergeant said, 'You are utterly unscrupulous and think you can play fast and loose with young women of good character and destroy their lives.'

2 MAY

1906 Until it was cut down in 1906, a venerable, spreading tree known as Maud's Elm stood in Swindon Lane on the outskirts of Cheltenham, a reminder of the tragic seventeenth-century legend of Maud Bowen.

3 MAY

Maud's Elm was felled in 1906.

MAUD'S ELM.
THE LAST OF THE OLD TREE. THE STUMP NOW ONLY REMAINS PROTECTED BY RAILINGS ERECTED BY CHELTENHAM CORPORATION.

MAUD'S ELM.

[The photo of Maud Bowen's Elm, Cheltenham's legendary tree, of which this is a copy, was apparently taken when the tree was not very much past its prime.]

The tree grew from a stake thrust through Maud Bowen's heart.

Maud lived with her mother Margaret in Swindon Village. Just turned 21, she was handsome, kind of heart and industrious, as heroines in woeful legends often are. The Bowens were spinners, and it was while taking the fruits of their labours to market in Cheltenham that Maud met misfortune.

When she failed to return home by nightfall, anxious Swindon villagers set out to search and at first light discovered the girl, face down in a stream, drowned. On a nearby bridge a second corpse was found; it was Maud's uncle Geoffrey with an arrow through his heart, fragments of his niece's dress clutched in his dead hand.

The lord of the manor appointed a coroner to investigate, who soon returned the verdict that Maud had murdered Geoffrey and then committed suicide. The order was given for Maud's body to be buried at the nearest crossroads with an elm stake driven through her heart. From this stake the tree grew that bore her name.

Some while later Maud's mum was sitting beside her daughter's grave when the heartless lord and his entourage passed by. One of the lord's men tried to move Mrs Bowen on, but an arrow from the bow of an unseen archer struck him down. The villainous lord declared that Margaret Bowen was a witch and ordered her to be burned on her daughter's grave.

On the day of execution Margaret was tied to a stake and the kindling at her feet lit as all the while the lord of the manor tormented her. Then at the height of the inferno's fury the fire fell in on itself with a supernatural crash. When the smoke cleared Margaret Bowen had disappeared and the leering lord lay dead on the ground with an arrow through his heart.

Years later a lonely old man moved into the Bowens' cottage, venturing from it only occasionally to sit in contemplation at Maud's graveside. His name was Walter Baldwin, and in his youth he had been Maud's sweetheart. On his deathbed Walter revealed the truth of what had happened on the fateful night, long before, when Maud met her mysterious end.

The lord of the manor, it transpired, lusted after Maud and enrolled her uncle Geoffrey to help him abduct the girl on her way home from Cheltenham market. When attacked by the wicked duo, Maud let out a scream, which was

heard by Walter, who was hunting nearby. Rushing to protect his love Walter shot and killed Geoffrey, but the evil lord escaped, while Maud swooned, fell into the stream and expired. Walter it was who dispatched the attendant that rough-handled Margaret Bowen. And Walter it was who killed the real villain of the story, the lascivious lord, at Margaret's execution.

4 MAY **1471** On this day the Battle of Tewkesbury was fought, the final and decisive action between the houses of York and Lancaster in the Wars of the Roses. Led by Queen Margaret of Anjou, wife of the imprisoned Henry VI, and her son Prince Rupert, the Lancastrians were caught in a pincer movement and routed. Their massacre took place in what came to be called Bloody Meadow.

Some 3,000 of the 5,000 Lancastrian army were killed on the field of battle, or cut down as they tried to flee by crossing the river at Abbey Mill. A number of nobles managed to make the crossing and sought sanctuary in the Abbey church, but twenty-one of them were summarily tried and beheaded at Tewkesbury Cross.

5 MAY **1912** The *Southgate Recorder*, church magazine of Southgate congregational church, Gloucester, informs us that Abraham Rice & Sons offered 'monuments in marble, stone, or granite erected at any distance', while butchers George Greenwood and John Newth, both of Northgate Street, were noted for their pickled tongues.

6 MAY **1858** *Cheltenham Examiner*: 'Death of Mr. Charles Fowler, for many years one of the leading physicians of the town. Mr. Fowler had retired from practice for some time, a disease of the brain having incapacitated him for the active duties of his profession. On his retirement an address, numerously signed, was presented to him, the document being enclosed in a casket of exquisite design and elaborate workmanship, made expressly for the occasion. It was formed of solid rosewood, richly ornamented with filigree work and silver, having on a silver plate a copy of the address and appropriate inscription. It was surmounted by a statuette group in frosted silver, being a facsimile of the Good Samaritan standing in the vestibule of the Cheltenham Hospital.'

7 MAY **1952** In May the *Gloucestershire Echo* reported that a chicken belonging to Mrs Lynes of Greenway Lane, Charlton Kings, had produced an egg weighing 8oz and measuring 3¼in long by 8½in in circumference. If you're wondering what is so grim about that, spare a thought for the chicken.

8 MAY **1861** *Cheltenham Examiner*: 'Death in the midst of a dreadful storm off the coast of Ireland, of Captain Boyd of HMS *Ajax*, and brother of the Revd Canon Boyd, late incumbent of Christ Church. Captain Boyd, with a number of his men, was throwing a rope from the shore to the drowning crew of a vessel, when a huge billow engulfed him in its recoil and carried him away before the eyes of his companions. The body was recovered after some days and honoured with a public funeral, and a tablet to the memory of the deceased has been erected in the church which for so many years was hallowed by his brother's ministry in Cheltenham.'

9 MAY **1904** The illustration you see reproduced opposite is taken from the *Gloucestershire Graphic* and illustrates a local legend – the sea serpent of Coombe Hill. The story goes that many years ago a sea monster swam up the

THE·SEA·SERPENT· OF·COOMBE·HILL·

A sea monster terrorised Coombe Hill.

Severn and settled on the bank of the river at Coombe Hill. From there it terrorised the local community, at first merely hunting sheep and poultry, but soon extending its diet to include human babies and milkmaids. Forty-odd feet in length, the wriggling mass of bone and gristle wrought such panic that all inhabitants in the vicinity fled. The saviour of the situation was a bright, local lad named Tom Smith. He left tasty titbits, such as roasted pig, for the monster to snack upon, and gradually won its affection. Eventually the serpent was eating from Tom Smith's hand, and while it was doing so one day, chomping on a marrow bone, the local hero bashed the sea snake over the head and killed it stone dead. Tom was rewarded by the local community with limitless free beer.

10 MAY **1899** In the ebbing years of the nineteenth century many of Gloucester's great and good took their last journey courtesy of Ernest Goodwin. This city undertaker operated from premises at 222 Barton Street. Ernest's success was based on specialisation. His main competitor was the Co-op, which had very cleverly cornered a big chunk of the burying business by offering funerals on the never-never. What actually happened was that people paid 6d a week, year after year, while they were alive. Then when they eventually shuffled off this mortal coil they did so with the peace of mind that they owed no one a penny.

The Co-op did well out of this scheme, and Ernest Goodwin realised he could not compete at this end of the market. So instead he raised his sights, and his prices, and became Gloucester's funeral director to the wealthy and celebrated. Goodwin was the first city undertaker to equip himself with a motor hearse. Handcarts and horse-drawn hearses might be alright for the hoi polloi, but Mr Goodwin's clients made their final journey in a specially converted Morris Cowley Bullnose. This impressive vehicle even had pump-up tyres which, had the honoured passenger inside been in a condition to appreciate it, did much to reduce the bump and jolt of that cobbled era.

On one glorious occasion, Ernest Goodwin had a particularly eminent customer in the back of his Bullnose Morris. To emphasise the standing of the person lying in the hearse, Ernest personally lead the cortège on foot up what is now Eastgate Street, but was then Barton Street. Resplendent the proud funeral director looked in black shiny top hat, tailcoat and, above all, a cast-iron demeanour of professional respect and respectability.

And so the procession processed, slowly and with dignity, towards Barton Gates, where the railway crossed the road. Ernest crossed the crossing, looking neither to left nor right, and therefore unaware that the gates had shut behind him, blocking the progress of the cortège in his wake. On he walked, up the middle of Eastgate Street towards the Cross, unaware that his ambition to be way out on his own in the funeral business had been realised.

11 MAY **1812** In the early nineteenth century the land now occupied by Cheltenham's Promenade was a marshy bog, boasting nothing more impressive than a few rather ramshackle cottages. In one of them the widow of Spencer Percival came to live after her husband had the dubious distinction of being the only British Prime Minister to be assassinated. He was shot on this day by a Liverpool banker named John Bellingham, who was hanged for the crime eleven days later.

1935 In Wyck Rissington church can be found a plaque 'In memory of James **12 MAY** Loveridge of no fixed abode (Gypsy). Entered into rest this day. Aged 48 years. Gone but not forgotten.' Loveridge died while travelling through the village and, in accordance with gypsy custom, his caravan and possessions were burned on a nearby hill. Presiding at the funeral was Canon Harry Heals who planted an allegorical maze in the rectory garden after being instructed to do so in a dream. The elaborate maze with 7ft-high hedges and 700 yards of paths became his life's work, but not long after the canon's death in 1984 it was demolished to make way for a housing development.

1649 St John the Baptist's Church, Burford, served as a prison to some 340 mutinous Levellers from the Parliamentarian army, who were held there for four days after being rounded up on the evening of this Sunday by Oliver Cromwell. Three of the ringleaders were shot but, in a rare display of benevolence, Cromwell let the fourth go after he had made a speech of penitence.

The churchwardens were furious that the building had been used as a place of incarceration; not because they were offended by the church being put to so secular a use, but because the recently repaired roof was damaged. They also objected to meeting the cost of cleaning up after the prisoners.

13 MAY

Burford church was prison to mutineers.

1845 This day the *Cheltenham Examiner* reported on the ancient and annual **14 MAY** practice of beating the boundaries. 'Parish boundaries perambulated. The procession was headed by the Parochial authorities and a band of music. At one place a man had to go up a ladder, through a window and out at another window in the back of the house as the boundary was supposed to run through the premises. When the procession reached the Golden Valley the followers, 2,000 in number, were treated with beer and cider ad lib.

'In the course of the proceedings Mr. J. Douglas, a retired tradesman, who was just recovering from a severe fit of illness, was looking on at the procession when a fellow named Pulham came behind him and pushed him into the deepest part of the Chelt. Pulham's conduct led to fatal consequence, for the immersion caused such a shock to Mr. Douglas's system as to hasten his death.'

15 MAY **1856** When the Great Western Railway was forced by commercial pressures to abandon its broad gauge tracks, the company was left with a lot of useless rolling stock. In this month an auction took place in Gloucester when the following lots were offered: seven first-class carriages, five composites, six second-class carriages, six third-class carriages, three carriage trucks, three horse boxes, one passenger engine, one goods engine, twenty-nine high-side wagons, eight low-sided timber wagons and one six-wheeled timber truck. There were no bidders at the sale.

16 MAY **1858** The newly launched *Tewkesbury Register and Gazette* gave an account of the brisk breeze that visited town on this day in 1858: 'This Sunday morning about 1 o'clock, a storm of terrific violence, though of short duration, passed over the town. An invalid boy had his bed covered by a complete avalanche of debris of the building. On his removal to the Hospital it was found that a piece of flesh, three inches in length, had been removed from his shoulder; and, embedded in the wound, a small piece of his shirt was found. His face, chest, arms and abdomen were much grazed and one eye completely closed, the loss of the sight being at first apprehended. Fortunately he recovered, ultimately without any permanent injury.'

17 MAY **1908** In the early years of the twentieth century the Wagon Works in Gloucester supplied carriages for the Imperial Russian railway system. The first batch of rolling stock was completed and had been in service for a time when the Bristol Road firm received a request from the Russian railway authorities. They requested that the type of grease being used in the axle boxes of the carriages be changed, as the vegetable lubricant used in the first batch of rolling stock was being eaten by peasants, causing the axles to seize up.

Peasants ate axle grease from railway carriages.

1858 *Cheltenham Examiner:* 'Mrs. Hewson, wife of Dr. Hewson of Warwick House committed suicide by poison. Deceased had been but lately married to Dr. Hewson and committed the act in a fit of insanity.'

18 MAY

1874 On this day Gilbert Jessop, one of the hardest-hitting batsmen in the history of cricket, was born in Cheltenham. In 1902 he rose to celebrity by hitting 104 in seventy-seven minutes against Australia in a test at the Oval. Jessop's playing days were unfortunately brought to an abrupt end when in 1916 he was left for too long in a heat treatment cabinet, which rendered him unable to work again for ten years.

19 MAY

Hard-hitter Jessop was stumped by heat treatment.

CHELTENHAM CHRONICLE AND GLOUCESTERSHIRE GRAPHIC, JUNE 15, 1907.

THE GLOUCESTERSHIRE ELEVEN
THAT DISMISSED NORTHAMPTONSHIRE AT GLOUCESTER ON JUNE 11, 1907, FOR 12 RUNS, THE LOWEST SCORE EVER RECORDED IN FIRST CLASS INTER-COUNTY CRICKET
Standing: Milward (umpire), Parker, Langdon, Spry, M. G. Salter, Huggins, Wrathall, West (umpire).
Sitting: Board, Dennett, G. L. Jessop (captain), R. T. H. Mackenzie, E. P. Barnett.

1924 The *Citizen* carried a graphic report of a freak deluge which inundated Brockworth. 'Not for 50 years have we experienced such a torrential downpour, accompanied by lightning and thunder. Observers declare that the flood advanced down the main road from Witcombe and Brockworth with every appearance of a miniature Severn bore, the head of the flood being at least a foot in height.'

20 MAY

Passengers on a tram at Barnwood were stranded when a wall of water engulfed the vehicle. Poultry drowned, orchards were uprooted and English's rose nursery in Upton Lane lost almost all of its stock.

Mrs Saunder of The Bungalow, Green Lane, jumped up onto her piano as the flood swept into her house. Not until water was lapping at the keyboard did the level begin to drop.

21 MAY **1954** Perhaps the most curious timepiece in the county looks down from the tower of Tirley church. This was made in the early years of last century from a selection of scrap – door hinges, skittle balls, bits of a threshing machine and what have you – by an ingenious local chap known as 'Old Cal'. Old Cal religiously wound his eccentric clock day after day for half a century and it kept perfect time. But when the Grim Reaper called Cal on this day, the old clock called 'Time' and no amount of coaxing would restart its ticker.

22 MAY **1941** HMS *Gloucester* met its fate during the Battle of Crete. The destroyer HMS *Greyhound* was sunk, and *Gloucester* was one of four ships ordered by Admiral King to rescue survivors. While en route, *Gloucester* was jumped by German dive bombers and suffered a number of direct hits. These brought the ship to a halt, its deck smashed and fires raging. Out of a crew of 804, only eighty-one were saved, of whom eighty were taken prisoner. Those on board were reported to have sung 'Abide with me' as the ship went down.

23 MAY **1987** Tewkesbury boasts a good collection of old trade signs above its retail premises. One that can be seen over the door of a shop in the High Street is the traditional red-and-white-striped barber's pole, which was put back into position on this day after being restored. Picturesque though it seems to us today, the origin of this symbol is pretty gruesome. It is a graphic recollection of the time when barbers also practised phlebotomy – blood-letting. The pole represents the wooden stake that was gripped by the person whose vein was about to be slit. The red stands for the blood, and the diagonal white stripes remind us of the bandages that were applied afterwards.

24 MAY **1735** According to legend, when Gloucester Cathedral was being built, a 14-year-old boy apprentice fell from the scaffolding to his death. His ghost, it was said, continued to haunt the site and building work was impeded. Consequently an exorcism was arranged. The priest who conducted the ceremony on this day is said to have coaxed the boy's spirit into a leather bottle, which was then sealed inside one of the mighty pillars that line the nave.

25 MAY **1846** The ancient stocks at Ashchurch, which were last used on this day, can be found adjacent to the path that leads to St Nicholas's church. They were positioned so that, in an age when everyone went to church, any miscreant locked in the stocks would be certain to receive maximum ridicule and universal condemnation by the community.

946 Edmund I, King of the West Saxons, was celebrating the feast of St 26 MAY
Augustine with his entourage at Pucklekirk (now Pucklechurch) when he
spotted a gatecrasher named Leolf among the gathering. Edmund asked the
uninvited guest to leave the gathering; he replied to the request by drawing
his dagger and stabbing His Majesty to death. The King's followers looked on,
too drunk to intervene.

1964 Robinswood Hill is so named because Robin Hood stood on it and 27 MAY
threw stones at the Devil. That is the legend, but the truth is less picturesque.
The land was leased from the crown by a local family named Robins. It was
also heavily wooded, hence Robinswood. The original name, however, was
Mattes Knoll. 'Mattes' is an ancient British word meaning death, and reminds
us that a burial mound once stood on top of the hill.

1847 *Cheltenham Examiner*: The Commission of Lunacy sat at the Belle Vue 28 MAY
Hotel to enquire into the state of mind of Commodore Beattie of Keynsham
Place. The jury found that the unfortunate gentleman had been of unsound
mind since 28 May 1845.

1940 The Battle of Cassell, which reached its climax this day, has been called 29 MAY
the forgotten last stand of the Second World War. It was fought by the
Glosters under Lt Col Michael Duncan and, but for its success, the evacuation
of Dunkirk could not have taken place.

  Cassell is a small town some 20 miles from Dunkirk. It was at this spot that
the 2nd Glosters, already under-strength, were ordered to hold back the
German advance. With the 1st Buckinghamshire Regiment the
Glosters held an 11-mile line that stretched from Cassell to
Hazebrouck. Against overwhelming odds, including heavy tanks,
the local regiment held their ground and fought to the last round
of ammunition. The majority of those who took part were either
killed or taken prisoner.

1860 An advertisement was issued by the churchwardens of 30 MAY
St Mary's parish church in Cheltenham on this day,
inviting tenders for concreting the nave. When the
old floor was removed two ancient stone coffins
were discovered. In filling up the grave the
Cheltenham Examiner states that 'in one of the
vaults, that of an old and well known
inhabitant of the town who died about
20 years ago, the wood of the coffin was
in a perfect state of preservation, the
polish on the wood was undimmed and
the metal of the coffin plate, handles & c.
was as bright as ever'.

Coffins discovered
beneath the floor.

31 MAY **1930** The inadequacies of Bishops Cleeve's own fire brigade were demonstrated in 1930. The village's fire engine had been in service since the early years of Queen Victoria's reign. This prized item of equipment had solid tyres, was horse-drawn and was kept in a lean-to shed at the side of the thatched cottage in which lived Charlie Trapp, the chief fireman.

In an emergency, villagers rushed off to Charlie's cottage with details of the blaze and its location. Charlie then jumped on his bike to ride round Bishops Cleeve and muster his crew of four, who dutifully gathered back at the chief fireman's house. Then the horse was brought in from the field, harnessed up to the century-old engine, and off the brigade went to fight the flames. Needless to say, the worst of the fire was usually over by the time they arrived.

Fire engine was past sell-by date.
(Tim Carr)

On this day Oldacre's mill caught fire. Charlie and co. were summoned, Charlie got his bike out, harnessed the horse and so forth, and when they eventually arrived on the scene the fourth-division fire-fighting force faced a Premier League inferno. Brigades from Cheltenham and Gloucester were contacted, but as Bishops Cleeve parish council did not subscribe to their maintenance, neither turned out to help. Stroud volunteer brigade did, however, provide assistance. Its limitations exposed, Cleeve's antique fire engine was put to rest in an outbuilding near the tithe barn.

JUNE

✦

In 1938 'John Collins' Midget Circus' arrived in Gloucester and pitched its small top on the Oxleaze. An advertisement in the Citizen billed this spectacular as 'The world's largest midget circus' and also as 'The only one of its kind in the world'. (Well, if the latter claim were true, the former had to be.) Some twenty-three miniature entertainers rode bareback on zebras, cracked whips over cowering lions, forced dogs to jump through hoops of fire. And to present-day thinking, it's difficult to conceive of anything less politically correct. The longest day of the year falls on 21 June and is the excuse for all manner of odd behaviour. A contributor to the Gentleman's Magazine in 1783 described the occasion in Randwick, near Stroud. Villagers elected a mayor for the day, who was seated in an armchair and borne aloft with some ceremony. The mayor in the chair was then deposited in the middle of the village pond, where he sat while all around gathered to sing a long and solemn song.

1 June **1846** An express train travelling from Bristol to Birmingham had reached Berkeley Road when one of the engine's wheels came off. The whole train left the rails and the first carriage was demolished, but miraculously nobody was injured.

Seven years later a broad gauge GWR goods train stalled just outside Gloucester. The driver and fireman jumped down from the footplate and walked towards the rear of the train, intending to uncouple a few carriages and lighten the load. Lucky for them they did, because the locomotive exploded with such violence that the top section of the boiler shot high in the air, flew over a row of cottages and landed 500 yards away.

2 June **1940** During the Second World War the tower of St Bartholomew's Church on Chosen Hill saw service as a signal station for the Home Guard. Messages were sent from this vantage point to units at Rotol and the Gloster Aircraft Company, at first by Aldis lamp, then by field telephone, and eventually wireless.

In this month, with the Dunkirk evacuation just completed and the likelihood of a Nazi invasion believed imminent, people in Churchdown were stopped in their tracks by the sound of the church bell, and thought it was being tolled to announce the arrival of enemy paratroopers. A collective sigh of relief came when the true reason for the alarm was revealed. An over-enthusiastic member of the Home Guard, who had misheard the radio message that 'Jersey' had been invaded, believed 'Dursley' had been overrun.

3 June **1838** June has proved to be a bumper month for surprising catches along the Gloucestershire Severn. In 1838 a 228lb sturgeon was caught between Gloucester and Tewkesbury, and a 29lb pike was hooked at the same spot shortly after. In 1839 a walrus appeared in the river at Gloucester, and was promptly shot.

Ten years later a 21ft bottle-nosed whale was netted at Haw Bridge. Then in 1885 a 69ft whale was stranded on a sandbank at Sharpness and declared a hazard to shipping. A 50ft whale suffered the same fate in 1925. Further back in the records book we find reference in 1786 to an 11ft whale caught in the Severn, which was presented to Dr Jenner – the physician and naturalist – who lived at Berkeley.

Dr Jenner had a whale of a time.

1731 Hailstones the size of tennis balls fell on Cheltenham, killing livestock and causing £2,000 worth of damage to property. On this day a century later the River Chelt burst its banks and most of the town was inundated.

Killer hailstones rained down on livestock.

1789 More inclement weather was recorded on this day by the landlord of the Bell public house in Barton Street, Gloucester, who noted in his diary 'an intense frost and thick snow'. Snow also fell in Gloucester on 2 June 1944.

1786 The inaugural meeting took place of the Town and Paving Commissioners in Cheltenham, established by Act of Parliament to regulate the town's sanitary affairs. A report of the time tells us, 'The sewerage

Snow fell in Gloucester in June 1944.

was in a dangerous position. In the borough was situated 6,541 houses, out of which number only 736 were belonging to the Cheltenham Sewers Company, so that upwards of 5,000 houses had no legal outlet and might be compelled to stop up their drains and have resort to the contaminating practice of cesspools. These private sewers mostly emptied themselves in the Chelt, and so polluted the stream (once so celebrated for its purity as to yield fish in quantity) that effluvia arising from it rendered it a public nuisance.'

7 June **1939** At 9 a.m. on this day Ralph Smith, aged 41, was hanged in Gloucester prison. He had the dubious privilege of being the last person to be executed in the city.

Smith's was a crime of passion. While living in Swindon earlier during the year he had become besotted with his landlady, Beatrice Baxter. The affection was not returned, and when Beatrice declared she was going out to meet another man, Smith snapped and stabbed her in the neck with a razor.

A crowd of over 100 gathered in silence outside Gloucester prison on the morning of the execution. The gruesome task was performed by Thomas Pierrepoint, assisted by Albert Pierrepoint, for which the father and son team received the fee of £10 plus travelling expenses. Dr Graham, medical officer for the prison on that day, reported that Smith gave no trouble.

8 June **1923** The death was reported of Jimmy Teague, Hucclecote's last village blacksmith. Mr Teague was a member of the parish council and a firm believer in actions speaking louder than words. On a number of occasions when fellow councillors failed to share his point of view on a particular subject, he took his jacket off, showed his biceps and challenged them to step outside.

A Hucclecote resident told the story of how Mr Teague had saved a man's life. 'One day at the abattoir on the Green [Mill Hay] my grandfather the local slaughterman slipped on some blood while he was pole axing a steer and Jimmy hit the animal between the eyes and knocked it out. He then picked up my grandfather and took him to a place of safety and returned to finish the job off for him.'

After a long period of illness, during which he had not been able to work, Mr Teague was found hanging in his smithy.

9 June **1796** John Paine, a Cheltenham blacksmith whose embers were extinguished in this year, was recalled by the inscription on his tombstone in the parish churchyard.

> My sledge hammer lies reclined,
> My bellows pipe have lost its wind,
> My fire's extinct, my forge decayed,
> And in the dust my vice is laid.
> My coal is spent, my iron's gone,
> My nails are drove, my work is done.

1841 Tewkesbury Corporation approached the county council to ask if its
eleven prisoners could be accommodated in Gloucester gaol. The county
agreed, on condition that Tewkesbury Corporation paid half-a-crown a day for
each prisoner's upkeep. Tewkesbury replied that it was only prepared to pay
1s 6d and the wrangle continued for some time. Eventually, in 1854, a
compromise was struck when Tewkesbury agreed to pay 2s per prisoner per
day, and from that time the town was without a gaol of its own.

1856 The inscription on a tomb in St Peter's Church, Leckhampton, reads
'Frances Money Evans, aged 26, Fanny Rowlands, aged 2. Frederick Gambier,
aged 5 months, the wife and children of Henry Lloyd Evans, Major XV11th
Regiment, Bombay Infantry.' All died together at Cawnpore, being crushed by
the fall of the roof of the barracks, struck down by cannon fire on the
sixteenth day of the siege.

Leckhampton
churchyard contains
many tombs of men
who left England for
the exotic promise of
India and died on
arrival.

1837 The architect who designed Pittville Pump Room was released from the
county gaol. John Forbes was his name, and his life was a riches-to-rags story.
Forbes opened his practice in Cheltenham in 1820, and was highly successful.
He was commissioned to make alterations to the churches of Holy Trinity and
St Mary's, he designed St Paul's Church and William Pitt engaged him to
design the new Pittville estate.

Forbes grew rich on the proceeds and owned property all over town. But
then a series of unsuccessful building speculations thrust him deeply into

debt, and he had to sell everything, including his own home at 31 Montpellier Villas, to survive. Besides business problems, Forbes suffered personal tragedy when his two infant sons died within a short time, followed by his wife, who was 37.

Forbes' final fall came when he tried to pay his meat bill to a butcher in Winchcombe Street using a forged signature. After some months in gaol awaiting trial, Forbes pleaded not guilty to charges of forgery and attempting to defraud. Friends who were magistrates and solicitors gave character references in court, but even so the disgraced architect was found guilty and sentenced to transportation to Australia for life. This sentence was later commuted to a stretch in prison.

When he came out he returned to Cheltenham, began work again, remarried and had a daughter. No happy ending though: Forbes fell heavily into debt once more, the marriage went wrong, and he left town alone and penniless, never to be heard of again.

13 JUNE **1941** Painswick's rural tranquility suffered a cruel blow during the Second World War when, on this early June morning, bombs rained down on the village. Poultry Court (then lived in by a Mr Lewis), a house in Friday Street and another in Tibbiwell Lane all received direct hits. Four homes were destroyed in the raid, seven suffered serious damage, and a further thirty-five had windows blown in, or tiles blown off the roof. Electricity and telephone lines were severed. Ten people were injured in the bombings and two children were killed. Both of them, with sad irony, were evacuees who had been billeted in Painswick for their own safety.

14 JUNE **1857** According to information published in the *Gloucester Journal* on this day, public lavatories first appeared in Gloucester in about 1300. Local authorities recognised that travellers arriving in the city might be in need of a comfort stop, so latrines were erected at the city gates.

At the North Gate (which was positioned at the corner of present-day St John's Lane and Northgate Street) a convenience was positioned over Fullbrook Stream. The watercourse then flowed through the precincts of St Peter's Abbey, to the displeasure of the monks who lived there. In 1372 they lodged an official complaint, declaring that the pong from the Fullbrook was so strong at the height of the summer that it put them off their prayers.

15 JUNE **1660** A plague of frogs descended on Fairford after a downpour of rain on this day. The amphibians swarmed all over the town. This was said to be an act of God by

A plague of frogs fell on Fairford.

the congregation of local dissenters, whose services had been frequently interrupted by 'a company of Rude People' who disapproved of their beliefs. They complained to the local JP William Oldisworth who warned the rude people not to be so unkind. This done, the frogs vanished as quickly as they had appeared.

1857   Another reference to lives lost in the Indian Mutiny can be found in St Peter's, Leckhampton, dating from 1857. 'For 21 days 900 British and loyal Indians, nearly half of them women and children, were besieged and attacked by 3,000 sepoys with the Nana Sahib at their head. At length on 16th June they were granted safe conduct. As they were leaving by boat they were fired upon and all the men were killed, the women and children were cut to death with knives and their bodies thrown into a well.'

16 JUNE

Gravestone in Leckhampton churchyard.

1858   'Thunder storm. St. Margaret's, the residence of Captain Smith, struck by lightning and much damaged; and a young lady, Miss Boteler, standing at the window at Monson Villa, struck down and rendered insensible.' (*Norman's History of Cheltenham* by John Goding, published 1863)

17 JUNE

1940   This day, a Tuesday, a single Luftwaffe Heinkel bomber attacked the Bristol Aircraft Company works at Filton with a brace of high-explosive bombs. They missed, but injured two airmen who were stationed at a nearby barrage balloon site.

18 JUNE

19 June

Cholera was a killer due to Tewkesbury's sorry sewers.

1882 Until adequate sewers were installed in Tewkesbury, cholera was a regular visitor. After an outbreak this year killed fifty-four people, the *Tewkesbury Yearly Register* noted, 'The disease was principally confined to the humbler classes of society.' Indeed it was. Over half of the seventy-six fatalities were from the families of stocking makers and labourers, and a quarter of the dead were children under ten.

At that time the town's residents disposed of their human and household waste into one of eight open drains that served the town, and into these same gullies went refuse dumped by butchers and other businesses, the effluent from water closets, plus the slops from Tewkesbury's two public conveniences. This unwholesome blend

PUBLIC HEALTH ACT
(11 & 12 Vict., cap. 63).

REPORT

TO THE

GENERAL BOARD OF HEALTH

OF A

PRELIMINARY INQUIRY

INTO THE SEWERAGE, DRAINAGE, AND SUPPLY OF WATER, AND THE SANITARY CONDITION OF THE INHABITANTS,

OF THE TOWN AND BOROUGH OF

TEWKESBURY,

IN THE COUNTY OF GLOUCESTER.

By THOMAS WEBSTER RAMMELL, Esq.,
SUPERINTENDING INSPECTOR.

LONDON:

PRINTED BY WILLIAM CLOWES & SONS, STAMFORD STREET,
FOR HER MAJESTY'S STATIONERY OFFICE.

1850.

was washed into the Avon and the Swilgate, the same rivers used by the majority of local residents for their domestic water supply.

As late as 1940 a County Council survey revealed that, in times of flood, Tewkesbury sewerage works were submerged, allowing raw effluent to enter the Severn less that a mile from the Cheltenham and Gloucester Water Board's intake for water.

20 June

1843 George Stokes Esq., one of the founders of, and chief writers for the Religious Tract Society, died suddenly at his residence in Cheltenham. The notice of his death states, 'So calm was his end that not a ruffle of the bedclothes gave evidence of any mortal struggle.'

21 June

1894 To see a steeple that is close to being perfectly proportioned, go to St Paul's Church in Shurdington. Slender and handsome, it rises to 109ft and has been struck by lightning on a number of occasions, most seriously on this day in 1894. As a result, much of the structure had to be rebuilt.

According to a local folk tale, St Paul's steeple caused a man's death.

Perfect proportions of Shurdington steeple.

The story goes that when the builder of the steeple at nearby St Peter's in Leckhampton was unable to match the perfection of Shurdington's spire, he took his own life in shame.

Leckhampton builder aspired to perfection, but failed. *Left:* A carving of the Green man in Shurdington Church.

1856   The church at Shipton Sollars is unique in the county for the fact that the chancel is a few inches lower than the nave. Chancel and nave were at one time on a level, but no right of burial was attached to the churchyard at Shipton Sollars, so that over the years the number of bodies interred beneath the nave was sufficient to raise it literally on the bones of the departed. Nave burials at this church ceased on this date.

22 June

1856   A Crimean soldier named Seymour died of lockjaw in Cheltenham workhouse. He was wounded at the Alma, and public indignation was strongly expressed at his being discharged on the beggarly pension of 6*d* a day, and thus allowed to end his days in the workhouse.

23 June

1965   The Rollright Stones are found not far from Chipping Norton. According to local lore, a king in ancient times set out to conquer England

24 June

and was met at this spot by a witch who pronounced 'Seven long strides shalt thou take, if Long Compton thou can see, then king of England thou shalt be. If Long Compton thou cannot see, then king of England thou shalt not be.' For a reason that the legend does not make clear, the witch then turned the would-be monarch and his followers into stones. (Taken from the *Gloucester Journal* of this date)

25 JUNE   **1547**   Catherine Parr, the sixth wife of Henry VIII, came to Sudeley when the King died in this year and married her former lover Lord Seymour. She died in childbirth the following year, and is buried in the grounds of the castle.

Sudeley is the final resting place of Catherine Parr.

26 JUNE   **1830**   On this day George IV shuffled off this mortal coil. The *Cheltenham Examiner* reported 'A great storm and flood occurred on this day. Its effects were very similar to those of the storm last Thursday last, except that the waters then swept through fields instead of through streets.' The River Chelt burst its banks and carried off the potato crop of a Mr Russell, who farmed land about where the Municipal Offices stand today.

27 JUNE   **1851**   *Cheltenham Examiner*. 'Died at Cheltenham James Hastings, known in the neighbourhood as "Hunting Jim" and to readers of Bell's Life as "The flying tailor". Jim became enamoured of the sport and always went on foot, invariably refusing a mount, and with stick in one hand and the other hand in his trowser pocket he would top the highest fence and be in at the death after the hardest run. It was a common occurrence with him to walk from Cheltenham to Berkeley, 25 miles, from thence, to meet and follow the hounds all day, be in at the death and walk back to Cheltenham in the same night!

'Another of his feats was still more wonderful. The meet being at Broadway, Jim got up early in the morning, walked from Cheltenham to Broadway, 16 miles, thence to the cover side, 8 miles, ran with the hounds all day and was in at the death, at Fairford, 12 miles, back to Broadway, 20 miles, and thence to Cheltenham, 16 miles; as though this was not sufficient, Jim again joined a badger hunting party to Queens and West Wood, at least 12 miles more, making the distance accomplished, between sunset and sunrise, 84 miles!'

The dolphin is a motif seen on various buildings in Tetbury, including the weather-vane that tops the Town Hall turret. It reminds us that a member of the de Breuse family, who were lords of the manor, was once on a ship bound for Ireland when the vessel was holed and began to sink. Much praying was done by de Breuse and crew, whereupon the ship stopped sinking and reached land safely. On inspection it was discovered that two dolphins had wedged themselves into the hole in the ship's side, sacrificing their lives so that the local lord was saved.

Dolphins sacrificed themselves to save Tetbury noble.

1848 *Cheltenham Examiner.* On the night of the poll at the Cheltenham election a voter named Mulcock, a fly proprietor, left his home, and next day his body was found in the stream near Pittville Lake. A prolonged enquiry was made into the circumstances, but the mystery was never solved.

Mystery of dead fly proprietor was never solved.

30 June **1612** Captain Robert Dover, with royal approval, arranged a Gloucestershire version of the Olympic games at Dover's Hill, Aston-sub-Edge. The idea took off, and within a few years had become the biggest organised sporting occasion in England. Events included gurning (face pulling) and there was a prize for the person who could recite the longest poem. But the biggest attraction for spectators was the shinkicking competition. Contestants prepared for this weeks in advance by beating their shins with planks of wood to harden them up. Then, on the day of the contest, combatants in pairs held one another by the shoulders and, wearing heavy boots, took it in turns to kick the other's shins.

There is no mincing of words in this *Citizen* report of 1910.

OUTING OF POOR CRIPPLED CHILDREN OF GLOUCESTER
(TO SHARPNESS TEA GARDENS, JUNE 18th, 1910).
Organised by Adult Schools' Union. President. H. Money; Secretary, F. W. Viner; Treasurer, J. Embling.
(Photo by Leonard E. Hopkin, 9 Midland

JULY

✠

We tend to think of Cheltenham as a genteel resort. But even at the height of its fashionable spa fame, there was a guttersnipe side to the town. Cudgel matches were staged regularly in the High Street, especially on long summer evenings. This simple sport involved men armed with heavy clubs knocking one another senseless. A poster of the time tells us that 'A good hat and a guinea in money' awaited the contestant who broke the most heads in three bouts. Cock-fighting and bull-baiting were other popular pastimes. Cheltenham was by no means unique in its liking for such brutal sports. Cirencester's impressive amphitheatre, a leftover from Roman times and the largest in Britain, was able to accommodate about 9,000 people. The earthwork construction is known locally to this day as the Bull Ring, a reminder that bull-baiting was a popular spectacle with locals in the eighteenth century.

1 JULY   **1853**   *Cheltenham Examiner.* 'Garrotte robbery in Cheltenham. A gentleman named Raymond, residing in Lyppiatt Terrace, was throttled under trees near the house of Lord de Saumarez, and while in a state of insensibility, his watch, purse and umbrella were stolen from him. The umbrella was picked up next morning, but the watch and purse were not recovered.'

2 JULY   **1969**   Cheltenham-born Brian Jones, guitar player and multi-instrumentalist member of the Rolling Stones, was found drowned in the swimming pool of his home in Hartfield, Essex.

Rolling Stone Brian Jones (centre) was found dead in a swimming pool. (*Photograph Michael Charity*)

3 JULY   **1845**   A severe hailstorm in Cheltenham and its environs was recorded. 'The High Street was flooded and several other thoroughfares rendered for a time impassable', read one report in a local newspaper. 'In the conservatories of Lord Sudeley at Toddington, eight thousand panes of glass were broken by the hail, and at Hewletts, Wormington Grange, and other exposed localities, the damage was very serious.'

4 JULY   **1832**   Tewkesbury fell victim to a cholera epidemic, the first of a number of visitations that plagued the town during the nineteenth century. The disease swept through the alleys that stretched behind Barton Street, Church Street and the High Street, not abating until the following September. As ever, the

great majority of the victims were from the lower orders. The last recorded death was 23-year-old Margaret Jones, a prostitute.

1937   An episode of *in situ* butchery is recalled in this ditty from *Nursery Rhymes of Gloucester City*, which you may (depending on your vintage) remember singing in school.   5 JULY

> There's an ox lying dead at the end of the lane,
> His head on the pathway, his feet in the drain.
> The lane is so narrow, his back was so wide,
> He got stuck in the road twixt a house on each side.
>
> He couldn't go forward, he couldn't go back,
> He was stuck just as fast as a nail in a crack,
> And the people all shouted 'So tightly he fits,
> We must kill him and carve him and move him in bits.'
>
> So a butcher dispatched him and then had a sale
> Of his ribs and his sirloin, his rump and his tail;
> And the farmer he told me, 'I'll never again
> Drive cattle to market down Oxbode Lane.'

1932   Customers at the Bell Inn, on the village green at Frampton-on-Severn, must have wondered if the landlord had been putting something extra in the cider that day when they saw an airborne saveloy pass over the pub. The soaring sausage was, in fact, the *Graf Zeppelin*. The German dirigible continued to London where it welcomed aboard fee-paying passengers, then embarked   6 JULY

Fortunately a photographer was on hand when the *Great Zeppelin* overflew the Bell Inn in 1932.

upon a 24-hour flight round the coastline of Britain. Officially this was a sightseeing trip. Actually it provided a splendid opportunity to take aerial photographs of Britain's coastal defences, which the Luftwaffe found enormously useful a few short years later. This must be one of the few instances in history when people have paid to help an enemy airforce bomb them.

7 JULY **1893** Until this month, when Cheltenham's first public abattoir opened in Gloucester Road, there were thirty-five private slaughterhouses in operation in the town. This fact was bemoaned by successive medical officers. They pointed out that the smell, drains clogged by discarded offal and infected meat were not conducive to the well being of local residents. In an earlier attempt to curb these difficulties, it was from the mid-sixteenth century forbidden to dump animal skins and carcasses into the River Chelt.

8 JULY **1851** *Cheltenham Examiner*: 'Extraordinary accident on the Great Western Railway. An excursion train from Cheltenham to London was ascending the steep incline up the Stroud valley and, when in the middle of the Salperton tunnel, the coupling irons gave way, and a number of the carriages, freed from the first portion of the train, commenced running backwards down the incline. The mail train was ascending on the same line of rails, and the driver (Wilkinson) seeing the runaway carriages coming towards him, at once, with great presence of mind, commenced backing his own engine and allowed the carriages to cushion safely against his own engine and so saved the excursion passengers from imminent peril.'

9 JULY **1553** Gloucester has the rare distinction of being a city in which both a king and queen have been crowned. In 1216 the coronation of 9-year-old Henry III took place in the cathedral, in rushed circumstances. Consequently there was no crown for the young monarch, who instead had his mother's bracelet placed on his head. On this day Lady Jane Grey was crowned Queen of England – at the New Inn, Northgate Street. (Has any other British monarch been crowned in a pub?) Lady Jane reigned for just nine days; then Mary Tudor had her head cut off.

10 JULY **1644** King Charles I checked into the White Hart in Moreton-in-Marsh after the Battle of Marston Moor. No doubt he was feeling glum, because things were not going well in the Civil War. His army had just lost 4,000 men, with another 1,500 captured. Things, of course, worsened for the king and as a reminder of his connection with the town the chair and footstool used by the doomed monarch at the trial prior to his execution was at one time on display at Moreton's Cottage Hospital.

11 JULY **1855** A news report described two days of remarkable rain experienced by Cheltenham when 'the water actually hissed as it fell upon the pavement. The water of the Chelt burst its banks and rushed through the town in a deluge. In a very few minutes the whole of the houses from the Bath Road to Alstone, and occupying a belt of some hundred yards in width, had their basements flooded from three to four feet in depth'.

The 1-acre site of a coal and faggot wharf at Charlton Kings was washed away. Then the torrent swept down into Sandford fields (now the park) carrying away fences, pig-sties, hay ricks and garden produce. On the water raged, flooding the Prom 'with the velocity of a mill race and carrying away several venturesome pedestrians who attempted to ford it'. The weight and impetus of the 100-yd-wide wall of water burst the banks behind York Terrace, decimating an ornamental nursery named Jessops' Gardens (now the Jessop's Avenue car park) and drowning a large number of specialist poultry.

1788   On this day George III arrived in Cheltenham to take the waters on the advice of his doctors; he was accompanied by Queen Charlotte, their three eldest daughters, and royal hangers-on galore. The previous month the King had suffered what he described as 'A pretty smart bilious attack' and had been advised by his doctors that the health-giving qualities of Cheltenham waters would have the sickly sovereign fit and well again in two shakes.   12 JULY

In fact the unfortunate monarch was suffering the early stages of a rare genetic disorder called porphyria. Besides biliousness, he displayed such first symptoms of this disease as irritating rashes, cramps and difficulty in breathing. Then came the onset of pronounced mood swings, so that George burst into tears for no apparent reason, and soon after chattered away like a mad thing. The illness developed quickly. An equerry who kept a diary of the King's progress along the road to insanity recorded that George had talked non-stop for nineteen hours until his voice was hoarse. Perhaps worst of all, George knew his state of mind was in decline. 'I wish to God I might die,' he told his son Frederick, 'for I am going to be mad.'

Shortly afterwards he attacked his son over dinner, before suffering convulsions and falling into a coma. A specially designed chair, which in lucid moments he referred to as his throne, was made to restrain the King. In less lucid, more manic moments George was confined in a straitjacket and subjected to cures prescribed by his physicians, such as having his skin blistered so as to let out the excess body heat. He died, deaf, blind and mad in 1820.

1852   A curious natural disaster befell Mr and Mrs Taylor this evening. The Taylors were market gardeners by trade, and were making ready for bed at their home in Rowanfield, near Cheltenham, after a hard day's market gardening, when the first crashes of thunder broke overhead. Mr Taylor was already in bed, while his wife knelt at her prayers, when in through the open window shot a fire-ball. The sizzling phenomenon passed between Mrs Taylor's legs, then struck the bed causing it to collapse (and presumably Mr Taylor to fall out). The fireball then collided with the wall of the house, which also collapsed, making the roof fall in. When the dust settled, the cottage was virtually demolished. Mercifully though, no injury was caused to the Taylors (except for singed thighs in the case of Mrs T.), or to their children who had been asleep in the adjacent room.   13 JULY

14 JULY   **1941**   Staverton was bombed by the Luftwaffe. A Dornier 215 dropped three devices from 8,000ft that killed two airmen and injured other staff. No damage was done to the intended target – the parked Wellington, Halifax, Whitley and Hurricane aircraft.

15 JULY   **1840**   Kid Wake, who sounds like a character from the Wild West, but in fact came from Gosport, was sentenced to five years' hard labour in Gloucester gaol for shouting rude slogans at George III during the monarch's visit to the city.

16 JULY   **1840**   Sir William Russell suffered an unusual accident while hunting at Charlton Park, Charlton Kings. The press report read: 'Sir William and Mr. Ibbertson, of East Court, had mounted one of the trees in the park for the purpose of shooting a deer, when Sir William, in attempting to descend, fell a distance of 10ft, and falling on his head, sustained a severe concussion of the brain, and was for some time insensible.'

17 JULY   **1791**   When it opened on this day, the new Gloucester gaol was considered a breakthrough in prison reform. In 1777 John Howard published a report called 'The state of the prisons', which painted a grim picture of life inside. Overcrowding, squalor and filth abounded. At that time Gloucester's old County Gaol was housed in the keep of the old Norman castle and facilities were non-existent. There was no bath, no medical provision; a rudimentary sewer deposited human waste in an open mound near the entrance, and the building was so dilapidated that prisoners had to be chained up at night to prevent them escaping through holes in the walls. Typhus and smallpox were so rife that for every prisoner who was executed officially, three died of disease.

Old Gloucester gaol was rife with disease.

1852 More inclement weather struck Cheltenham this month. 'An unusually close and sultry day. Rain descended not in drops, but as though poured bodily out of some reservoir above.' Then came the hurricane 'sweeping away everything movable and prostrating everything permanent which stood in its way'.

18 JULY

Pigsties were unroofed, walls flattened, chimneys blown down, and a wooden house on Marle Hill plucked from its foundations and flung 300 yards. In the same vicinity, a slaughterhouse belonging to Mr Warner was demolished, while a tree on his neighbour's ground measuring 70ft in height, 25ft across its roots and 18ft in circumference of the trunk was uprooted. (*Norman's History of Cheltenham* by John Goding, published 1863.)

1921 The Gloster Aircraft Company competed in the Enfield Aerial Derby. The company's entry was a streamlined Mars 1 Bamel biplane, designed by H.P. Folland. At the controls was GAC test pilot Jimmy James. Preparation of the locally built plane did not go without a hitch. One problem was the 440hp Napier engine, which tended to cut out due to fuel starvation when the plane turned. Even more serious was the hot and rainless summer of 1921, which had caused cracks to open up in the grass airstrip at Brockworth. Just one week before the prestigious air race was scheduled to take place at Enfield, the Mars 1 Bamel was taken out for trials and was accelerating to take off when the tailskid dropped into a hole in the runway. This resulted in the back end of the aeroplane being pulled off.

19 JULY

Gloster plane was not a high flier.
(*Photograph from* The Best *by John Whitaker*)

20 JULY   The story of St Margaret, who is closely associated with Bentham, tells the tale of a double life that ended in singular misery. The daughter of a nobleman, Margaret was forced to marry against her will. But rather than suffer the marriage to be consummated, she fled on her wedding night, disguised as a man and, calling herself Pelagius, entered a monastery.

So exemplary in conduct was Margaret that she was eventually made priest in charge. But things began to go awry when a nun in a nearby convent fell pregnant, and the fickle finger of suspicion pointed at Pelagius as the pater. As punishment, Margaret was walled up and left until dead. Only after she had expired was Margaret's lifelong secret revealed, presumably to the surprise of many and the particular chagrin of those who had ordered the brickwork. St Margaret's day is 20 July.

21 JULY   **1926**   On its twenty-fifth anniversary, the Cheltenham coiffeur Foice's published a booklet detailing the up-to-date equipment to be found in its Promenade salon. Notable on the inventory was a steamer device into which the client's head was inserted so that 'The pores of the skin are opened and blackheads and other facial blemishes can be removed without inconvenience.'

22 JULY   **1841**   Benoni Hill, landlord of the Bull Inn, Gloucester, died. Dubbed the city's greatest wit, Mr Hill downed twenty-eight pints of his home-brewed beer day in, day out. Given the circumstances, he had done well to reach his 54th birthday.

23 JULY   **1842**   Cheltenham's MP, Craven Berkeley, fought a duel with another Member of the House, Captain H.G. Boldero. This was spurred, according to Berkeley, by Boldero making 'certain expressions disrespectful to Her Majesty'.

In time-honoured fashion the two met at dawn in Osterley Park. Berkeley's second was W. Ridley Colborne and Boldero's W.E.F. McKenzie, both of whom were also Members of Parliament. Pistols were chosen. The two stood back to back, walked ten paces, fired, and both missed. The procedure was repeated, and both missed again, whereupon they left the park and went about their usual business.

24 JULY   **1910**   Pioneer aviator Ernest Willows passed over Blakeney in his hydrogen-filled airship. It says much about life in the Forest of Dean at the time that a local was prompted to write a letter to the *Gloucester Citizen* declaring, 'Altogether it is tolerably certain that there has not been such an exciting five minutes in Blakeney perhaps since the world began.' Willows, by the way, was killed in an air crash in 1926.

25 JULY   **1940**   South Cerney airfield was attacked by two German bombers, and on the same day local people caught sight of the enemy in the air for the first time when a Luftwaffe Ju88 flew low over the area. This could have been the same plane that was later brought down at Oakridge Lynch, near Stroud, when it was rammed by a Hurricane of the Kemble Defence Flight, killing its pilot Alex Bird.

1863 Belas Knap, near Winchcome, is a neolithic long barrow, 170ft long and built in about 1500BC with a false end, perhaps to try and fox graverobbers. In this year archaeological excavations took place, and thirty-six ancient skeletons were discovered.

26 JULY

1912 John Albert Matthews' furniture factory in Llanthony Road, Gloucester, caught fire in 1912. Flames rapidly engulfed the building and spread to High Orchard and Exhibition Street, destroying the homes of fifteen families. Wind-borne sparks carried to Walet Colwell's livery stables in Luke Street, and soon the mews was ablaze too. The 200 men who lost their jobs when Matthews disappeared in flames suffered the additional blow of losing all the tools of their trade.

27 JULY

It is said that Stroud folk would never accept food in Painswick, because they believed residents there ate 'Bow-wow' pie, a delicacy made from stray dogs.

28 JULY

1763 In the churchyard of St Mary, Chipping Norton, is an unusual gravestone in memory of Phillis Humphreys, who died at the age of fifty-eight this year. The inscription describes her as a 'Rat catcher who has lodged in many a town and travelled far and near. By age and death she is struck down to her last lodging here.'

29 JULY

The names of Lower Slaughter and its near namesake Upper Slaughter may suggest a bloodthirsty episode in the history of their surroundings. The truth, however, is far less fearsome. Some old guidebooks claim the name derives from the sloe (or black-thorn) tree, but it more likely comes from 'slough', meaning a muddy place.

30 JULY

31 JULY **1854** Uley tumulus, a neolithic burial place, yielded twenty-eight human skeletons when the site was excavated in 1854. A mile north is another long barrow, quaintly named Hetty Pegler's Tump. The story goes that in the seventeenth century the land on which this ancient monument stood belonged to a woman of this name who enjoyed nothing more than to sit on the pagan grave and sing.

Hetty Pegler's Tump, Uley.

AUGUST

✠

The phrase about life hanging on a thread has particular poignancy in the case of the young woman whose story is told in the chapter to come. She died of embroidery. Then for proof that life can be full of surprises we have the tale of a rent collector named Harrison who was going about his business in Chipping Campden and by an unusual turn of events was sold into slavery by Turkish pirates. Never a dull moment for some. August being a warm and sultry month, everyday life must have been trying for residents of Cheltenham's Swindon Place (which ran between the Lower High Street and Swindon Road). Demolished in the 1930s, this bijou development of des. res. back-to-backs was described by a Board of Health inspector as being 'without sewerage, carriageway or pavement: the gutter channels on the surface are always full of filthy fluid; and the place is never free from fever. Wanting in ventilation, the houses are always in an unhealthy condition.'

1 AUGUST **1940** Unlikely but true is the Tewkesbury tale of how a First World War field gun killed a man during the Second World War. In the early 1920s a captured German artillery piece was presented to the people of Tewkesbury in recognition of their fund-raising contributions to the war effort. The gun was placed in Victoria Pleasure Gardens, and there it stayed until the Second World War when it was removed, along with other ironwork, for scrap. While the weapon was being dismantled, its recoil spring was released by mistake, shot out of the barrel and dislodged a few slates from the roof of a nearby house. A little later, when a workman arrived to make good the damage, he fell from the roof and was killed.

2 AUGUST **1835** Local farmer Joe Thompson arrived at Gloucester market in August with two lots to sell: a Newfoundland dog and his wife. Mr and Mrs Thompson had marched up the aisle three years before, but, according to Joe, the marriage was not one made in heaven: 'She's been a born serpent,' he told the amused market-day crowd. 'I took her for the good of my home, but she has become my tormentor. A domestic curse. A nightly invasion and a daily devil.' The crestfallen farmer then offered this advice: 'Avoid troublesome women as you would a mad dog, a roaring lion, a loaded pistol, cholera, Mount Etna and any other pestilent thing in nature.' The only (almost) good things Joe had to say about his spirited spouse were 'She can read and milk cows.' A city gent named Henry Mears offered Joe 28s for Thompson's wife and the dog. They shook on it and the deal was done.

3 AUGUST **1642** According to local tradition, when blood was first spilled in the English Civil War, the King's Head in Cirencester played a role in the drama. Lord Giles Chandos came to Cirencester to enlist men for the Royalist army. The townspeople, however, were by persuasion Parliamentarian and set about Chandos's party, burning his coach in Market Place and killing some of his followers. Chandos fled to the King's Head, where he remained until the crowd's bloodlust had subsided and he was able to make a prudent retreat.

Brass of armoured man and his faithful dog in Cirencester parish church.

4 AUGUST **1914** When war against Germany was declared in this year, Cheltenham, like most towns and cities throughout the country, was gripped by jingoistic euphoria. Recruitment rallies, such as those staged in the Town Hall and the Territorial Army Drill Hall in North Street (to the rear of where Littlewoods now stands), drew eager crowds. Throngs surged to open-air meetings at the Prom end of Clarence Street and, buoyed by the promise of glory and adventure, men young and not so young struggled to be first in the queue at the recruitment office. By the end of October 1914 over 1,400 locals had signed up.

Recruitment rally snakes past the Gordon Lamp, Cheltenham, 1915.

For many of them it was, indeed, all over by Christmas, just as the recruitment officers had promised. By the end of the war there were 1,600 names of people from Cheltenham on the roll of honour, from a town population of a little under 50,000.

642 Compton Abdale's church is dedicated to St Oswald, the Christian King of Northumberland who was slain at the battle of Maserfield on this day by Penda, the pagan monarch of Mercia. To make sure everyone knew who had won, Penda ordered Oswald's head, arms and hands to be cut off and displayed on stakes around the battlefield. A year later Oswald's brother Oswy collected his sibling's body parts and dispatched the head to Lindisfarne, where it was placed in the coffin of St Cuthbert. The hands and arms went to Bamburgh, and the torso was buried in Maserfield.

5 August

1800 Joseph Stephens of Minchinhampton was hanged at Gloucester gaol for stealing cloth.

6 August

7 August **1831** James Hammerton of Tewkesbury was sentenced to fourteen days' hard labour in the House of Correction for stealing bread, herrings and onions from the shop of Mr Charles Archer. William Smith, aged 13, and his 12-year-old brother were privately whipped for stealing turnips, and then discharged. Samuel Lewis was sentenced to seven years' transportation to Van Diemen's Land for cutting off and stealing the manes and tails of a colt and gelding, the property of Mr Aaron Pike of Mitton.

8 August **1843** Local newspapers reported that a smallholder named Mr Hughes who lived in New Street, Cheltenham had been blessed with a newly born calf that boasted eight legs, four ears and two tails, all of which were perfectly formed. What is more the animal lived into adulthood.

9 August **1814** Sarah Humphries, a *felo de se*, was buried at the crossroads leading to Swindon Village, the last instance of a crossroad burial in the parish. The deceased destroyed herself by drinking vitriol.

10 August **1633** On the wall of Chipping Campden church in the Earl of Gainsborough's mortuary chapel is an ornate monument in marble and alabaster to Penelope Noel, a young woman who died from blood poisoning after she pricked her finger while embroidering.

Monument to the dangers of embroidery in Chipping Campden church.

11 August **1966** Until the cattle market was moved out of Gloucester city centre to make way for the bus station in the 1960s, a striking advertisement for a local sausage-maker appeared on the end wall of a building that overlooked the square. It featured a smiling pig, pulling a line of linked sausages behind him, and the slogan read 'He's drawing his own conclusion.'

12 August **1783** The line of Sapperton Tunnel was marked out by Robert Whitworth. At 3,817 yards in length, the proposed construction, 15ft wide by 15ft high, was among the most ambitious civil engineering projects of its time.

Four tenders to build the tunnel were submitted to the committee charged with overseeing the project and the contract was won by Charles Jones. His first quote to build was eight guineas a yard, which the committee said was too expensive. Jones's second quote for six guineas a yard they declared too cheap. So he eventually accepted seven guineas and the work progressed, though not very well.

Charles Jones proved to be an unfortunate choice of contractor. Burdened by financial problems, often unwilling or unable to pay his workers, a noted imbiber and an inept engineer (the entrance to part of the tunnel collapsed),

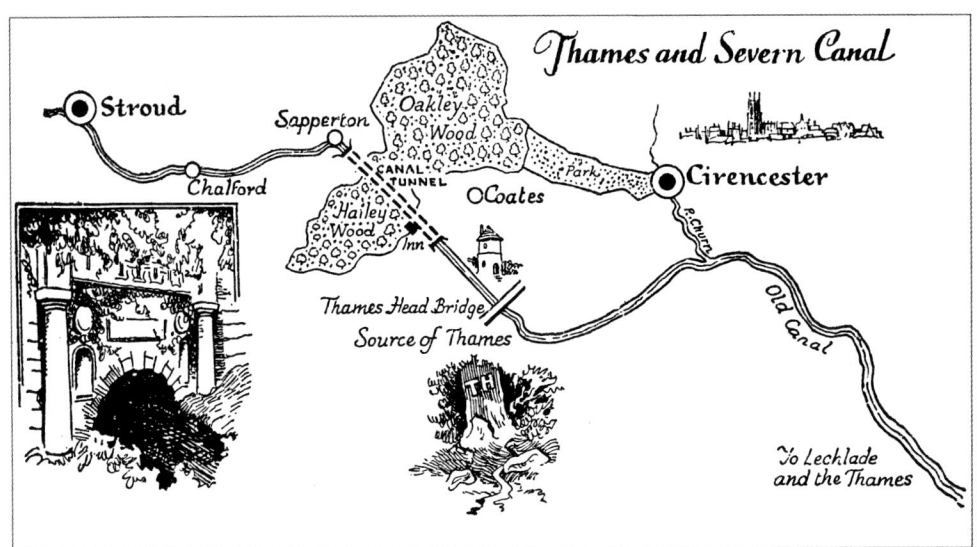

Thames and Severn Canal

Stroud · Sapperton · Oakley Wood · Cirencester · Chalford · Canal Tunnel · Coates · Park · Hailey Wood · Inn · Thames Head Bridge · Source of Thames · Old Canal · To Lechlade and the Thames

The contract to build Sapperton was awarded to a drunk, bankrupt, inept engineer.

Jones was given the elbow after his third spell in prison for failure to pay his debts. Among other reasons for dismissing him, the committee described Jones as 'Vain, shifty and artful in all his dealings'.

13 August

1855 *Cheltenham Examiner:* 'Mrs Dornier, a lady well known in Cheltenham, died from injuries received from her dress coming into contact with the drawing room fire at her residence in Lansdown Place.'

14 August

In Churchdown, among other places in Gloucestershire, the belief was held that it was not possible to pass comfortably into the next world from a mattress, or pillow stuffed with pigeon feathers. If there was any suspicion that a person about to depart this life might be lying in a bed thus stuffed, it was usual to take them from their bed and leave them to die on the floor.

15 August

1842 On this day at Gloucester Assizes, George Jacob Holyoake was found guilty of uttering blasphemy at Cheltenham, and George Adams of selling blasphemous publications. Chief Justice Tindal sentenced Holyoake to six months' and Adams to one months' imprisonment without hard labour.

16 August

1855 Emily Byron, a relative of the poet, died at Elmstone Hardwicke at the age of 16. Her epitaph reads:

> From scenes now shrouded oft with woe
> From life's depressing cares
> The youthful form that rests below
> The God of mercy spares
> Short was the span of life decreed
> Few were the griefs within
> The spirit from the casket freed
> Hath winged its flight from sin.

17 August   **1873**   Charles Butt, who lived with his mother at Church Farm in Arlingham, shot and killed his lover Amelia Phipps after an argument. He was 22, she was 20 and worked as a housekeeper for Butt's brother. Butt was found guilty and sentenced to death on Christmas Eve. The execution took place in Gloucester gaol in January 1874.

18 August   **1940**   It was a Sunday. The evening was clear. Sergeant Bruce Hancock, 26 years old and almost at the end of his course at No. 6 Flying Training School, took advantage of the good conditions to notch up some night-flight time. Solo, he took off from the grass airstrip at Windrush, near Bourton-on-the-Water, which had been pressed into wartime service. He was at the controls of an unarmed, Avro Anson trainer.

Lights lined the runway, and in the blackout conditions that blanketed Britain they could be seen from a great distance. Their glow attracted the attention of a German Heinkel He111, perhaps on course for Bristol, which had been the Luftwaffe's target the previous night. The twin-engined raider swooped on Windrush and released a number of high-explosive bombs. Dusk was now dissolving into darkness, but onlookers on the ground were still able to see the Avro Anson being brought in to land by Bruce Hancock. He had been spotted by the Heinkel too. Attacking from above and behind, the German plane's machine guns barked, peppering the unarmed trainer.

What happened next was described by eye witnesses. Hancock doused the lights of his Anson and banked to port. Then as the Heinkel overflew him, Hancock pulled back the control column and rammed his Anson into the underside of the enemy. The German plane came down at Blackpit's Farm, Aldsworth near Northleach, and pictures of the wreckage appeared in the *Cheltenham Chronicle* and *Gloucestershire Graphic*. So did photographs of the military funeral given to the Heinkel's crew of four, all men in their twenties.

Bruce Hancock's body was found some distance away from the remains of the Anson. He had once told his brother-in-law that if he ever came under attack while piloting an unarmed plane, he would attempt to ram the enemy.

19 August   **1400**   A brass in St John the Baptist Church, Cirencester commemorates Reginald Spycer, wool merchant and husband to four wives. Spycer gained favour with the King and became a local hero in 1400 when he almost single-handedly quashed a revolution against the crown. In that year the earls of Kent and Salisbury joined forces with the aim of restoring Richard II to the throne. Arriving in Cirencester with the intention of mustering support for their insurgency, the brace of earls soon realised they had misread local loyalties. Led by Reginald Spycer, a posse of townsfolk arrested Kent and Salisbury, and the next day cut off their heads in Market Place. King Henry IV was so grateful that he made a gift of the earls' treasure chest to the town, gave an annual grant of deer and wine, plus a pension of 100 marks to the town bailiff. This windfall paid for St John's tower.

St John the Baptist Church, Cirencester, c. 1930.

1728 At Berkeley Castle Dicky Pearce, England's last court jester, died while midway through a performance. His tomb can be found in Berkeley churchyard with this inscription (a rather heartless one it must be said), attributed to Jonathan Swift.

20 August

> Here lies the Earl of Suffolk's fool,
> Men called him Dicky Pearce,
> His folly served to make folks laugh
> When wit and mirth were scarce.
> Poor Dick alas is dead and gone
> What signifies to cry?
> Dickys enough are still to come
> To laugh at by and by.

1660 This odd tale from Chipping Campden concerns William Harrison, who at the age of 70 set off to collect rents for his landowning employer. When he failed to return, a search was started, and 3 miles away at Charringworth his

21 August

comb and bloodstained neckband were discovered. Justice being harsh and swift in those distant times, the blame was put on Harrison's manservant, John Perry, who was promptly hanged, with his brother and mother for good measure.

The judge at that trial must have had egg on his face when William Harrison arrived back in Chipping Campden two years later. Asked to explain his disappearance the aged rent collector said he had been kidnapped by horsemen and sold as a crew member aboard a ship that was captured by Turkish pirates. Then he was sold again, this time into slavery, but managed to escape and stow away on a boat to Lisbon, from where he had worked his passage to Dover, and so home to the Cotswolds.

22 AUGUST **1901** Two trams trundled from Lansdown Castle to Cleeve Hill carrying VIPs and local notables, the first passengers to travel on Cheltenham's new light railway. Two days before the system was scheduled to open, a tramcar descending Cleeve Hill on a trial run went out of control and overturned at Southam curve, killing two workmen. It was discovered that wooden brake shoes for the American-made double-decker had not been fitted. As a result of the accident the Board of Trade agreed to grant the tram company a licence, on condition that only single-deckers were used on the Cleeve Hill climb.

23 AUGUST **1856** A report from the *Cheltenham Examiner* suggests that Britain has not always deserved its reputation for being a nation of wildlife lovers. 'A large bird continued perched upon the vane of the Parish Church from Saturday afternoon until Monday morning, when Mr. Hollis, gunsmith, brought a favourite rifle to the churchyard, and after about half a dozen unsuccessful shots managed to bring down the strange visitor from its elevated perch. It proved to be a large pigeon.' Only a few weeks before a cormorant had been shot in Winchcombe Street.

24 AUGUST At Bisley it was the custom until the end of the eighteenth century to bury the dead in fishtail-shaped coffins with the deceased's legs parted. It is also recorded that in Winchcombe a woman designed her own open-ended coffin, so that should the Devil slip in through one aperture, she could slip out of the other.

25 AUGUST **1643** During the siege of Gloucester, a red-hot cannonball passed through three houses in Westgate

Street to land in the bedroom of James Commeline, who lived at no. 30. Mr Commeline, who was an apothecary, had only recently arrived in Gloucester, seeking a quiet life after the religious strife of his native Holland.

1793 Mrs Blocksum passed away in Prestbury at the age of 103. The *Gloucester Journal* reported she had predicted that she would rise from the dead in a few days' time, 'and therefore declared that her coffin lid should be taken off when she was interred, which was performed agreeable to her request'. The *Journal* concluded, 'If the old woman should be as good as her word, our readers may depend upon hearing of it.'

26 August

1859 John Tinsley, a student at the Training College in Cheltenham, drowned while bathing in the Severn at Wainlodes Hill. His remains were interred in Swindon Village churchyard.

27 August

1890 Ivor Gurney led a tragic life. Born on this day in Gloucester, he became a cathedral chorister at the age of 10. When the Great War came, he volunteered for the 2/5th Glosters and fought at the Somme, Arras and Ypres.

28 August

His first book of poems, *Severn and Somme*, was published in 1917 to considerable acclaim. But it was as a songwriter that the local man truly excelled. He studied at the Royal College of Music and was a close friend of Ralph Vaughan Williams (who is buried, by the way, in Ampney Crucis churchyard). In his short lifetime Ivor Gurney penned over 200 songs, and noted musical critics declared him the greatest exponent of the songwriter's art since Schubert. A glittering career lay before him, but Gurney's experiences during the war affected the balance of his sensitive mind. In 1922 he was admitted to Dartford mental hospital, and there he died at the age of 47. The official cause of death was given as TB, the result of being gassed in the trenches.

1876 Before dying at the age of 92 in 1876, Charles Hillier of Uley, a veteran of the Peninsular War, in which he had lost both legs, recounted the occasion of a skeleton found in a local stream. It was thought to belong to a Scottish beggar, who had disappeared in suspicious circumstances some years before. The skeleton was propped up in the porch of the village church for three successive Sundays, as villagers believed that if the person who had murdered the beggar passed by, the bones would bleed and identify the perpetrator of the crime.

29 August

Until half a century ago it was common practice in rural parts to tell the bees if their keeper had died. In Aldsworth the new keeper was required to stand before the hive and chant 'Bees be said your master's dead and you must work for me.' At Great Rissington it was believed sufficient simply to knock on the hive three times and announce, 'Your master's dead.' In the Forest of Dean town of St Briavels it was the custom to pick up a bee hive if a funeral procession passed by.

30 August

The people of Whaddon did not have theirs.

31 AUGUST 1939 With Britain on the threshold of war, 49,000 gas masks were distributed to households in Cheltenham, but due to administrative error nobody in Whaddon received one.

SEPTEMBER

†

People of Cam with memories that reach back half a century or so may well recall eating sparrow pudding this month. For local folk, this was the month for bird batting. Batmen went abroad at dusk, equipped with a lamp, bell, net and sticks. The latter were used to scare birds from bushes. Confused by the light from the lamp and the bong from the bell our feathered friends took flight, only to be caught in the netting. They were then despatched, covered in pastry and cooked in a slow oven. Strictly speaking, the name sparrow pie wasn't an accurate description of the ingredients, as blackbirds, tits, crows and the occasional nuthatch probably ended their days in the local delicacy too. If sparrow pie doesn't tickle your taste buds, perhaps pig face will. Sounds yummy? Then make a note in your diary to visit Avening on the 29th of this month when villagers celebrate Pig Face Day in time-honoured fashion. This involves eating (and you may well be ahead of me here, dear reader) pig face. A must for Gloucestershire gourmets.

1 SEPTEMBER 1950 John Whitehead, a city bus driver, received a nasty shock when negotiating his double-decker along Barton Street on this evening. At that time the railway line from Eastgate Station, which stood where Asda is today, crossed Barton Street. John's bus was stationary on the level crossing when he noticed a train heading along the tracks in his direction. The runaway train crashed through Barton Gates, hit the bus and carried it along the line. After some distance the double-decker was pushed to one side as the locomotive continued on its way, out of control. By then one side of the bus was wrecked, along with the cab. Seats from the lower deck were wrenched from their fixings, but by good luck only two passengers were on board and neither was hurt.

Barton Gates, Gloucester, where a city bus driver and his passengers received a nasty shock in the shape of a runaway train.

The vehicle was repaired at the depot in London Road (now BBC Radio Gloucester) and returned to service. Strangely, the same vehicle was wrecked again the following year after colliding with a house in Grange Road.

2 SEPTEMBER 1651 This was a black day for Scotland and Charles II of England, who formed an unlikely alliance to meet Cromwell's forces at Worcester. The Scots invaders were routed and suffered terrible losses. So complete was the defeat that the Royalist side was unable to raise another army for a decade. After the debacle, Charles II fled to Bristol, stopping overnight at Coberley. Having not previously booked accommodation, the King and his entourage billeted themselves on the unprepared Rector Lewis Jones, who was 105 years old and must have been more than a little surprised when he answered the door.

1919 'Tragedy at Gloucester' announced the *Gloucestershire Graphic*, reporting a crime of passion. It concerned Matthew Rogers of 45 New Street, who returned home on Saturday night to find his wife, who suspected his infidelity, in a high state of agitation; so high in fact that she grabbed a razor and promptly cut his throat, killing him almost instantly. The incident no doubt left a lasting impression on the Rogers' neighbours, Mr and Mrs Barnes and their two children, who had popped round to no. 45 for a cup of tea and witnessed the entire event.

A jealous wife cut her husband's throat.

CHELTENHAM CHRONICLE AND GLOUCESTERSHIRE GRAPHIC, SATURDAY, SEPTEMBER 20, 1919.

TRAGEDY AT GLOUCESTER.

The murder of a young man named Matthew Rogers, of 45 New-street, by his wife, through jealousy, took place in Gloucester on Saturday night last. In the presence of a neighbouring couple, Mr. and Mrs. Barnes, and their little boy and baby, Mrs. Rogers cut her husband's throat with a razor, killing him almost instantly.

1.—The scene of the tragedy, No. 45 New-street, the home of the Rogers family.
2.—Mrs. Barnes' little boy (aged 13) and baby (aged 9 months), who were present when the tragedy was enacted.
3.—Mr. Barnes, the next-door neighbour.
4.—The three little boys of the deceased man and his wife, aged 11, 7, and 5 respectively.
5.—Mrs. Barnes.
A portrait of Mrs. Rogers, the accused woman, is on another page.

[Photos by Cheltenham Newspaper Co., Ltd

Death by traction engine.

4 SEPTEMBER   1903   A fatal road accident was reported by the *Citizen*. A traction engine towing a threshing machine from Newent was being driven by a Mr William Wilks across Over Bridge when suddenly the engine 'gave a jump and the steering wheel was jerked out of his hands' according to the assistant driver Mr Holford. The engine crashed through railings and toppled down the embankment, inflicting injuries on the unfortunate William Wilks who later died in the Royal Infirmary.

5 SEPTEMBER
Sheep had four and a bit legs.

1914   An unusual sheep sprouting a vestigial extra leg was born to farmer James Warne of Eastington.

6 SEPTEMBER   1939   At their first meeting since the outbreak of war, Cheltenham magistrates imposed fines on those who had infringed the blackout regulations. Miss Baylis, manager of the Majestic Hotel in

Park Place, claimed she had been unable to obtain enough material for the hotel's 200 windows, which was certainly true. All the town's stores had run out and declared that further supplies were not obtainable for the time being.

Less excusable was the case of the landlord of the Lamb Hotel in the High Street. Magistrates were told he had made no effort to cover his windows, but instead had served customers in the dark. At closing time, however, the lights of his public bar had been turned full on to make sure the customers had all gone home. He was fined £3.

7 September

1552 *Scandal rocked Shurdington.* At the Consistory (church) Court, villager John Kynge sought to divorce his wife Joan, alleging 'that she lived and still does live in the bonds of adultery'. Joan denied the charge, and witnesses were called. The first revealed that Joan and a man named William Lock, who had moved to Shurdington six months before, had been seen 'very suspiciously together at home as well as in the fields'. However, the witness concluded that they had not been observed 'in any towardness of misconduct'. The next witness told all present that Joan and William Lock had repaired to the ox house together. There they remained for half and hour. On leaving the ox house it was noted that Joan had 'straw about her shoulders hanging'. The straw detail seems to have tipped the balance of the case, for 'After sundrie cogitations Joan made full confession of adulterie'.

8 September

Thief took coins to bridge poverty gap.

1823 Tewkesburians gathered to celebrate the laying of the foundation stone of Mythe bridge which, it was widely believed, would make the town a main route way and increase its fortunes greatly. A special service was conducted

in the abbey, church bells pealed; there were processional marches, much flag waving and a formal dinner at the Hop Pole Hotel. The town had a fine time. Next morning, however, it was discovered that the recently laid foundation stone had been dug up in the night and the coins embedded in the mortar beneath it stolen.

9 SEPTEMBER   **1854**   The Revd Raymond, Vicar of Swindon Village, published a statement giving the number of miles walked by Mrs Webb, a poor woman of Boddington, in search of a Union doctor to attend her sick husband. Finding a Union doctor who would attend the sick without insisting on his pound of flesh in the mid-nineteenth century was plainly as difficult as trying to find an NHS dentist in the twenty-first. The unfortunate woman was forced to trudge 'To Tewkesbury and back, 12 miles; to Swindon and Cheltenham, 8 miles; ditto, ditto, 8 miles; to see Relieving Officer of Boddington, 2 miles; to Swindon and Cheltenham (twice more); total 46 miles.'

10 SEPTEMBER   **1816**   Richard Reynolds, Quaker and industrialist, who owned the foundry at Coalbrookdale where the world's first iron bridge was made (and still spans the Severn to this day), came to Cheltenham for the sake of his health, and died. He was 81.

11 SEPTEMBER   **1835**   This rhyme appears on the gravestone of William Harris, who died in September and is buried at Staverton.

> My coffin, my bed, my house and grave
> A little narrow room is all I have
> My body's rotten, but my soul is flown
> To take its rest in a world unknown.

12 SEPTEMBER   **1863**   There is something of Groucho Marx's quip that 'Reports of my death have been greatly exaggerated' about this entry in the chronology section of John Goding's *History of Cheltenham*, published in this year. 'Accounts received in Cheltenham of the suicide of Col. Prince, formerly well known in the town. He was a member of the Canadian Legislature and conspicuous in his services in quelling the rebellion of 1838. He shot a number of prisoners taken at that rebellion, and was supposed to have been driven to the act of self destruction by the odium of that act of cold blooded butchery.

(In reference to this entry, Mr. William Hollis, of Badgeworth, an intimate friend of the Colonel, writes us on 22 January 1863 that the report of Colonel Prince's death is altogether a mistake. Mr. Hollis says "The Colonel is not dead, thank God for it! but still living in his glory, a hale old man, with his well earned honours smiling happily around him.") '

13 SEPTEMBER   **1718**   The Rector of St John's, Elkstone, entered in the church register, 'Was buried Richard, one of the twin sons of John Bradly, slaine by a gunne shott off by a quick sighted marksman.'

1852 *Cheltenham Examiner.* 'Death of the Duke of Wellington. The news of the sad event was received in Cheltenham with every demonstration of unfeigned sorrow. On the following Sunday, the ministers, both church and dissent, improved the occasion by special addresses to their several congregations.'

14 September

Duke of Wellington

1904 At 7.30 on the evening of this day, a gas explosion destroyed a shop in Winchcombe street, Cheltenham, reducing it to rubble. The demolished premises stood directly opposite what is now the Odeon, but was then Highbury Congregational church. From this address Mr Challice conducted his business, an unusual combination of taxidermy and carpet cleaning.

15 September

When the dust cleared, the violence of the blast was revealed. Not only had the kapok been knocked well and truly out of Challice's shop, but the sturdy front door, blown from its hinges, was discovered across the road in the churchyard. Debris, including a selection of stuffed and part-stuffed animals, was scattered along the street. Fortunately, no major injuries were sustained, although a young woman was struck by an unidentified flying object.

Highbury Congregational Church.

The ladies of Highbury Congregational Church were not amused by the gas explosion at a nearby taxidermist's.

16 SEPTEMBER   **1848**   The local press reported a trio of fatalities on the railway at Churchdown. 'This afternoon a deplorable accident, by which three workmen on the line were killed, and two others seriously injured. The men were engaged on the line and were standing on the up rails counting the trucks in one of the Midland down trains, when the Great Western train from Gloucester came upon them unawares, and swept them down like a flock of sheep.

'The engine driver of the Great Western train blew both his whistles to appraise the poor fellows of their danger, but the noise made by the goods trucks prevented their hearing and it was impossible to stop the train until it had passed over them. The driver, seeing that he could be of no service without medical assistance immediately drove on to Cheltenham.

'Dr. Brookes, the medical officer of the Great Western Company, immediately proceeded on the pilot engine to the scene of the catastrophe. On arriving there, the scene which presented itself was too awful for description. The bodies of the sufferers were crushed and mangled in a shocking manner, so much so, that it was with the greatest difficulty the different portions were put together for conveyance to Cheltenham. The two wounded men were conveyed to the Hospital, and though shockingly mutilated, ultimately recovered.'

Churchdown railway station, scene of a trio of fatalities.

1707   Alice Little died 'aged near 100 years', and is buried at Elmstone
Hardwick beneath a stone that bears this inscription:

> Death in a very good old age
> Did end her weary pilgrimage
> And was to her an ease from pain
> An entrance into life again.

1831   Cheltenham's New Burial Ground in the High Street was consecrated
and opened at a cost of £4,500, which included the purchase of land and
erection of the chapel thereon. The sum was raised by loans from local
residents who were repaid by instalment, each receiving interest at the rate of
5 per cent on their investment.

The acquisition was necessitated because the graveyard around the parish
church was full up, as reported at the time. 'That portion of the churchyard
which terminates with the walk leading to Well Walk and Chester Walk, is
crowded with memorials of the dead, as is the church within; and from the
designs of some of the decayed stones, it is evident that the spot has been
used as a place of sepulchre ever since its first consecration.'

1741   The unfortunate episode of an innocent party wrongly hanged
unfolded when Dame Eleanor Bunt was discovered dead in bed in a pool of
blood at her home in Bull Lane, Gloucester. 'The deep spreading stain on the
sheet and counterpane showed she had perished by the hand of a murderer',
concluded the *Gloucester Journal*.

The finder of the body was a neighbour, Miss Jones, who told constables
she had heard screams. She also told them she had overheard Henry Sims, a
fellow assistant at the Westgate Street shop where she worked, plotting with
the deceased's maid Mary Palmer. She explained that Sims and Palmer
intended to do away with the dame, steal her wherewithal and with it set
themselves up in a shop in Mary Palmer's home town of Littledean.

Constables searching the premises found money, a gold watch, jewellery
and silver plate missing from the deceased dame's dwelling, plus a smear of
blood on the handle of the door to the room of Mary Palmer, which was
sufficient evidence to commit the maid to Gloucester gaol, accused of
murder.

At the trial the examining doctor told the court Dame Eleanor had died
from a single stab administered with significant force. Despite the fact that she
was a slight slip of a girl – and despite the fact that she protested her
innocence strongly – Mary Palmer was sentenced to death and three days
later was hanged.

Two years later police caught up with a gang of ne'er do wells in
Cirencester who were charged and found guilty of theft, murder and heinous
crimes galore. Shortly before his execution, one of their number confessed
that he and an accomplice had killed Dame Eleanor Bunt and made off with
her valuables. When the truth was out, Mary Palmer's remains were removed

from the grounds of Gloucester gaol, placed in a fine coffin and accompanied to a grand grave at the expense of the city fathers, accompanied by civic leaders, magistrates, the judiciary and a strong sense of collective shame.

20 SEPTEMBER **1864** Epitaph at Brockworth to Joseph Baldwin.

> All ye that pass this way along
> Pray think how sudden I was gone
> Death doth not always warning give
> Therefore be careful how you live
> While you are living call for grace
> Death cometh stealing on apace
> Peace to this soul and may he rest
> in joys eternal with the blest.

21 SEPTEMBER **1935** On this day a thunderball appeared in the Park, Gloucester. An eye-witness watching from Parkend Road described the strange phenomenon as about the size of a football and made of fire. It gave off intense heat and light and moved erratically, accompanied by a hissing noise. The unearthly orb tore up ground and lurched into a willow, destroying half the tree and hurling splinters a distance of 100 yards. Having spent its energy in this violence, the thunderball disappeared.

22 SEPTEMBER **1857** The *Cheltenham Examiner* took obvious pleasure in unveiling a skeleton in the cupboard of an unfortunate local woman. 'A woman going by the name of Martha Heath, and living at 16, Sandford Street, was found drowned in the Chelt near Barratt's Mill. Deceased was 83 years of age. We understand that, although the deceased went by the name Heath, her real name was Martha Probert. She was the wife of a man of that name, who was, in company of Thurtell and Hunt, engaged in the robbery and murder of Mr. Weare, whose death some thirty years ago caused so much excitement throughout the country.

'On that occasion Probert saved himself from the gallows by turning King's evidence. His two companions in crime were convicted and hanged and Probert was sometime afterward convicted of horse stealing, and the crime at that time being a capital offence, he suffered the same fate as his former accomplices. Mrs. Probert then took upon herself the name of Heath, and has since resided with her relatives in Cheltenham'.

23 SEPTEMBER **1776** On this day the execution took place of a footman named Joseph Armstrong, who poisoned the lady of a Cheltenham household who had discovered him stealing. Armstrong was hanged in Gloucester and his body brought back to Cheltenham to be hung in chains from a hastily erected gibbet on the Marsh (roughly where Wellington Square stands today). After an hour the gibbet broke and the body fell to the ground. A bodger was called in to repair the structure, then Armstrong's remains were left on view for a year, much to the annoyance of certain well-to-do types, as the Marsh was a fashionable place to ride out.

After a year the murderer's skull was purchased by a local doctor named Minster and the remainder of the skeleton by another physician named Newell. The gibbet was bought by the owner of a local residence named Clonbroock House and recycled as gateposts.

1742 Stanway churchyard is the final resting place of the remarkable Thomas Dover, who died in the village at the age of 82. Given his lifestyle, this was no mean feat. When he fell victim to smallpox, Dover (probably wisely) eschewed conventional medical advice and embarked upon his own cure. This involved opening his veins to let blood, spending long periods naked in an unheated room with the windows open, and drinking a huge volume of beer laced with sulphuric acid.

24 September

It worked. So, at the age of 40, Dover led a band of pirates to Peru where enough booty was liberated to make wealthy all who took part. On his way back from South America, Dover rescued Alexander Selkirk, who had been stranded on the island of Mas a Tierra for four years. The story provided the inspiration for Daniel Defoe's *Robinson Crusoe*.

Perky after his financially successful venture in Peru, Dover organised another party to plunder the town of Guayaquil in Ecuador. Again the pickings were rich, but Dover and his mercenaries made the mistake of spending the night in the local church, where plague victims had recently been buried. Within two days, 200 of Dover's men fell ill, but by imposing a strict regime of blood-letting and the application of dilute sulphuric acid, all but eight survived.

1964 The tiny village of Meysey Hampton, which lies between Cirencester and Fairford, boasts a number of features that seem quaint today, but also serve to remind us that life in days gone by was not innocently idyllic. In the church is an ancient alms box, hewn from a single block of wood, thus making break-ins more difficult. Chains hanging from the lectern originally secured the church Bible against pilferage. And tucked into the corner of the churchyard is a picturesque small building, once a watch house in the days when newly buried corpses attracted the attention of bodysnatchers.

25 September

1728 In the tower of Bagendon church can be found an unusual memorial to Giles Parsloe, who died in this year. From it we learn little about Giles, but a good deal about his son who, no doubt, chose the wording and paid for the tablet.

26 September

> A dutiful son I have left behind
> No man on earth could be more kind
> Than he was to me in my dying hour.
> He did for me that to his utmost powe
> Nothing was me denyd that I would have
> In hopes to keep me longer from the grave,
> But God was pleased because he knows best
> To ease my pain and take my soul to rest.

27 SEPTEMBER **1847** *Cheltenham Examiner*: 'Died at Torquay, Vice Admiral Sir Charles Dashwood KCB and GCTS, resident of Cheltenham. Deceased entered the navy in 1779 and was, at the time of his death, the last living officer of the *Formidable*, in which ship he served as aide-de-camp to Lord Rodney in the actions of 9 and 12 April 1782. He was thus sixty-eight years in the Navy, upwards of forty of which he served at sea.'

28 SEPTEMBER **1935** A bizarre railway accident happened on this day in 1935 when the driver of a late evening train into Gloucester unhitched his engine from its carriages and left the steaming leviathan in a siding near the GWR sheds. Unfortunately, he forgot to put the brakes on. As the driver jumped down from his cab to make his way home, the live loco began slowly to roll. It gathered momentum, and by the time they reached the buffers, at the end of the line, the hundred or more tons of mobile iron were unstoppable. Bursting through the buffers, the engine ate up a distance of open ground, then ripped through a line of railings. Over the pavement it continued, on across Horton Road – its wheels slicing deep furrows in the surface – to crash through a brick wall. The runaway train was eventually brought to a halt when it became embedded in the side of the Home of Hope. Eighteen girls were asleep in this institution for children in care, and fortunately not one was injured.

29 SEPTEMBER **1990** Villagers at Avening traditionally celebrated Pig Face Day on the Sunday after Holy Rood Day. Locals tucked into sandwiches made from slices of pig's face, and the delicacy was even distributed free to customers at the local pubs. Campanologists gathered to ring out the specially composed peal for Pig Face Day, and were rewarded for their efforts with dumplings made from apple and, of course, pig's face.

The event was said to celebrate an occasion recalled uncertainly in the village's collective memory when a fierce boar that had been behaving in a boisterous and intimidating way was killed, and by way of rejoicing the good people of Avening tucked into its face.

Interest in Pig Face Day petered out just after the Second World War, for a reason that is hard to imagine. However, an attempt to revive the custom in 1990 met with enthusiasm from local people, when a special service in the village church was followed by a concert, during which was served a meal with pig's face once more on the menu.

30 SEPTEMBER In Fairford parish church a series of misericord carvings glimpse domestic life as it was in centuries past. One shows a woman beating her husband over the head with a ladle.

Fairford parish church.

OCTOBER

✠

*Some brisk breezes have whipped across the county in Octobers gone by.
The* Cheltenham Examiner *recorded that during this month in 1851 a
hurricane hit town in which 'a chimney at the gas works was blown through the
roof of the building and the lead at the railway station stripped off like so much
brown paper'. Cheltenham's St James Station opened on 23 October 1847, not a
grim event in itself, but while the site was being developed a Bronze Age tumulus
was flattened and three ancient human skulls taken from it. These were then put
on display in Devonshire Street school. Read on and you'll come across the story
of a ghost said to roam abroad on certain nights on Newnham-on-Severn's
Victoria Hotel. According to the current manager (April 2004), it can be reported
that the ethereal presence is still actively in residence.*

1 OCTOBER **1921** The war memorial in Cheltenham's Long Garden was unveiled on this day. Presiding at the ceremony was General Sir Robert Fanshawe, commander of the old 48th Division, in which many local men had served. The huge crowd that filled the Prom comprised relatives of the fallen, ex-service personnel, regular and territorial soldiers, civic and other dignitaries and a group of 250 children whose fathers had not returned from the trenches.

A competition was held to design a war memorial for Cheltenham's Promenade. This one did not win.

2 OCTOBER **1850** *Cheltenham Examiner:* 'This day died at Woodford, near Berkeley, aged 93 years, Mr. James Ingram, proprietor of the Fox public house in that village. Mr. Ingram was the last survivor of the crew of the *Royal George*, which sank at Spithead in 1782. His escape was almost miraculous.

'He was below at the time that the vessel sank, but was fortunate enough to get out of a porthole. As he was swimming towards the shore, one of the people who were on board at the time of the accident, and who, like himself, was struggling for life, caught hold of one of his feet and dragged him towards the bottom. In attempting to free himself from the deadly grasp one of Mr. Ingram's shoes came off, and he was by this means released from his perilous situation. The other shoe he retained as a relic to his dying day. Before reaching the shore he saw a woman being buffeted by the waves and being an expert swimmer he brought her safely to land with him.

'Deceased was well known to the travellers by the old coach road from Gloucester to Bristol, as the coachmen used generally to pull up to allow their passengers to see the veteran whose life had been marked by so miraculous an incident.'

1846 *Cheltenham Examiner*: 'Longevity. There is at present residing in the pleasant village of Woodmancote the widow of a farmer and a servant who has been residing with her from her youthful days, whose united ages amount to 197 years, the mistress being 99 years of age, and the servant 98. The widow is deprived of sight, but otherwise in the enjoyment of good health. The servant is still active for her years and devoted in her attendance to her mistress.'

3 OCTOBER

1946 *The Quick and the Dead* is the autobiography of Bill Waterton, who joined the Gloster Aircraft Company as chief test pilot this month and lived on a houseboat in Tewkesbury. His salary was £1,000 a year, by the way.

During his time at GAC, Waterton flew a number of the pioneering jet aeroplanes made by the innovative Brockworth firm. Besides the well-known successes, such as the Meteor and Javelin, GAC embarked upon a few projects that failed to get off the ground. One such was the E1/44, dubbed by Bill Waterton the 'Gloster Gormless'. The 'tubby, trunkless, silver winged elephant of an aeroplane' did not get off to a good start. The first prototype was destroyed when it tipped accidentally from a lorry. Then the second prototype shook so violently in taxiing trials that its nose fell off.

4 OCTOBER

1850 *Cheltenham Examiner*. 'Death of the Rev. J.C. Egginton, of Wellington Villa. Deceased met with an accident when in putting his horse at a fence in the neighbourhood of Andoversford, the animal caught his foot in the top stones of the wall and rolled with his rider into the adjoining field. The injuries received were of so serious a nature as to cause his death.'

5 OCTOBER

1536 An impressive tower rising to 111ft at North Nibley commemorates the life of William Tyndale, who reputedly was born in the village in about 1494. A student at both Oxford and Cambridge, Tyndale translated the New Testament into English, which greatly annoyed the church authorities. He then roused the ire of Henry VIII by writing the alliteratively titled *Practice of Prelates*, which unwisely denounced the King's intention to divorce Catherine of Aragon and marry Anne Boleyn. The much miffed monarch arranged for Tyndale to be arrested in Vilvorde, near Brussels. There he was thrown into a dungeon and left for a year, 135 days before being tried and duly found guilty of heresy. On 6 October 1536 Tyndale was stripped of his vestments, executed by strangulation, then his body burned.

6 OCTOBER

The memorial at North Nibley to William Tyndale, who was executed for his religious beliefs on 6 October 1536.

7 OCTOBER **1832** Epitaph formerly found in St Catherine's churchyard, Gloucester:

> Here lies the body of Captain Tully
> Who lived an 105 years fully.
> And three score years before as mayor
> The sword of the city he did bear.
> Nine of his wives do by him lie
> And so shall the tenth when she does die.

8 OCTOBER October, an Old English word from the Latin *octo* meaning eight, was in Roman times indeed the eighth month of the year. A visit to the Corinium Museum in Park Street reveals that 2,000 years ago Cirencester was a pretty up-market address to boast (which, of course, it still is). The well-to-do enjoyed a sophisticated lifestyle with central heating, imported delicacies in the covered shopping mall, two local eye specialists and regular entertainment at the amphitheatre. If you were invited to a finger buffet in Roman times, by the way, stuffed dormouse was likely tobe on the menu.

9 OCTOBER **1860** Local press reports of 1860 tell us of an 'Accident to Major Mortimer. While shooting in the neighbourhood of Winchcomb, the gallant major's gun exploded, badly shattering the thumb and forefinger of the right hand.'

10 OCTOBER **1855** Dr Jeune, who was then Canon of Gloucester and later became Bishop of Peterborough, opened the coffin of Edward II. The unfortunate monarch was murdered in Berkeley castle in 1327 by having a furnace-heated iron thrust into his bowels via his anus. It is said, quite believably, that the King's cries could be heard many miles hence. (Incidentally, some while ago there

Edward II was well and truly done to death in Berkeley castle.

was a folk group named, amusingly or tastelessly according to choice, Edward II and the Red Hot Polkas.)

The lead-sealed, wooden casket was removed from its tomb on the north side of the Cathedral's choir, and for two hours Dr Jeune, with a few close colleagues, looked upon . . . well, annoyingly we do not know, as there is no record of what was found. Then the royal remains were sealed again and once more interred.

11 OCTOBER **1851** *Cheltenham Examiner:* 'Hurricane in Cheltenham. On Wednesday, this neighbourhood was visited by a storm of wind, which, at one time, was more severe than any we have witnessed here for many years. The avenue at the Old Wells presented the appearance of a perfect wreck, the space between the rows of trees being almost completely blocked up with fallen branches, while the pleasure grounds were completely strewn with smaller fragments.

'During the same storm one of the larger boughs of Maud's Elm were blown down, a chimney at the Gas Works was blown through the roof of the building, and the lead at the railway station stripped off like so much brown paper. This hurricane appears to have been part of the same storm which has strewn our sea board with wrecks and caused the loss of a great many lives.'

12 OCTOBER **1825** In the tranquil churchyard of St Paul's, Shurdington is a melancholic epitaph 'In memory of Joseph Jordon Clark, died aged 13':

> Treat softly passenger for doth lye here
> We hope an angel in a brighter sphere.
> The trampling of an horse did give me my death wound
> My father found me moaning, bleeding on the ground.
> My mother did bewail me, in the jaws of death.
> Within nine hours to God I did resign my breath.
> A sudden change, I in a moment fell
> I had not time to bid my friends farewell.
> A sudden change may happen to us all.
> My lot's today, to morrow thine may fall.

Shurdington tomb tells a sorry story.

1928 Local people were among the fatalities in an accident reported by the *Citizen* under the headline, 'Terrible train disaster at Charfield, Gloucestershire'.

13 OCTOBER

The daily mail train left Gloucester Eastgate station on time at 4.48 a.m. and had reached Charfield station 20 miles down the line towards Bristol, when it collided with a goods train that was being shunted into a siding. The force of the impact propelled three passenger carriages off the track into a road bridge, and then the whole mangled chaos caught fire. Fourteen travellers who could not be rescued died in the flames.

CHELTENHAM CHRONICLE AND GLOUCESTERSHIRE GRAPHIC, SATURDAY, OCTOBER 20, 1928.

TERRIBLE TRAIN DISASTER AT CHARFIELD, GLOUCESTERSHIRE.

A dreadful accident, by which 14 persons were killed and many injured, took place at Charfield, a L.M. & S.R. station on main Gloucester to Bristol line, 20 miles south of Gloucester, on Saturday last.   The mail train, which leaves Cheltenham at 4.27 a.m. and Gloucester at 4.48, was travelling fast through Charfield when it plunged into a goods train which was being shunted off the same line into a siding.   Three carriages were telescoped and thrown against the road bridge, and the whole of the debris caught fire, burning to death the injured who could not be quickly extricated.   Our pictures were taken on Sunday, when many thousands witnessed the scenes of clearing the line.
1.—Crane hoisting wrecked carriages from   3.—A mass of wreckage alongside the line.   new boots, overcoats, etc., left in a heap.
    under bridge.   4.—Damaged trucks near the bridge.   6.—L.M. & S. officials beside the charred
2.—An overturned goods wagon beside track.   5.—Looking at personal effects of passengers,   remains of a passenger carriage.
                                                    ["Cheltenham Chronicle" Photos. Copies 1s. and 1s. 9d. each, post extra.

Elegant but ill-fated. The Severn Railway Bridge.

13 OCTOBER **1960** When it opened in 1879, the Severn railway bridge was hailed as a major engineering feat of the Victorian age. Vessels on the river, however, always found it a hazard, and collisions were frequent. The fatal blow came in this month. A number of oil tankers were heading up the estuary bound for Sharpness that evening, among them the *Arkendale H* and *Wastdale H*. A thick blanket of fog was draped across the Severn, the tide was roaring in, and in these difficult conditions the two ships collided.

A great explosion gave way to flames that rose in a column higher than the bridge beneath, which the stricken vessels were now careering. First to strike was the *Wastdale H*, but the two tankers were fused together in the inferno, so the full force of their combined mass smashed into the bridge. Five crew members were swept away and lost their lives.

A picture of devastation was revealed when the sun rose on the sorry scene next day. One of the bridge's piers and two of its spans were gone. Another pier was leaning. The gas main that was carried over the bridge to Lydney was cut, as were telephone lines. The two burnt-out tankers had been carried down the estuary to run aground on the east bank.

Although the bridge was now badly damaged and disabled, its repair was perfectly possible. Fate, however, decided differently. Less than two years later another oil tanker, the *BP Explorer* passed under the bridge and was on its way to Sharpness when it capsized. All lives on board were lost. The upturned tanker, gathering momentum on the receding tide, dealt the bridge another blow.

Then, just two months on, a floating crane called the *Tweedledum and Tweedledee*, which had been brought from Liverpool to help in the repair of the bridge, broke its anchorage on a high flood tide. Tugs were despatched to try and take the drifting crane in tow, but almost predictably were unsuccessful. The crane collided with the bridge inflicting more damage. Faced with a repair bill of almost £300,000, owners British Rail procrastinated for six years before deciding to dismantle the once-splendid example of nineteenth-century engineering prowess. This Severn landmark disappeared in 1967, but a number of the spans were shipped intact to Chile, where they are in use today as a road bridge.

1868   Not far from the north door of St Peter's, Leckhampton, is the grave of Richard Purser, 'Died in this parish October 1868 at the age of 111.' The long-lived Leckhamptonian's epitaph is taken from the Book of Proverbs and reads 'The fear of the Lord prolongeth days.'

14 OCTOBER

Leckhampton's longest-lived resident?

1848   *Cheltenham Examiner*: 'Died, [in Cheltenham] at the advanced age of 76, Richd. Oglesvy, Esq., RN. Deceased was in the navy between forty and fifty years; was a master in 1804, and possessed at the time of his deathhis original appointment to HMS *Hydra*, on the 18 January 1805, with the signature "Nelson and Bronte" in the handwriting of the great naval hero.

'Capt. Oglesvy served under Lords Collingwood and Nelson, and with Sir Ralph Abercrombie. He was engaged at the Nile, at Trafalgar, and other great sea fights of the last war, and was present on board the Victory when the immortal Nelson received his death wound.

15 OCTOBER

'During his retirement from active service he led a quiet and secluded life, but he maintained to the last the friendship and esteem of those gallant spirits with whom, in more troublous times, he had "braved the battle and the breeze" in his country's service.'

16 OCTOBER **1822** *Sovereign*, one of the first steam-boats seen on the River Severn, was moored in Gloucester docks. Large crowds gathered to see the strange, sailless craft, among them an engineer named Ralph Dodd. While he was inspecting the push rods and pistons, the vessel's boiler exploded, badly scalding Mr. Dodd.

Back in London the unfortunate man's doctor advised him to convalesce in Cheltenham, where the waters would restore him to health. Not rich, Dodd walked from London to Cheltenham, and died on the day of his arrival.

17 OCTOBER **1847** Reports in the local press described the excitement of a 'Penance at the Parish Church. An exhibition fortunately of rare occurrence in these enlightened days, took place on Saturday last at the Cheltenham Parish Church. Throughout the week rumours had been afloat that some unlikely wight who had made rather too free with the fair name of his neighbours, had been ordered by the Ecclesiastic authorities to expiate his offence by doing penance in a white sheet.

'It was asserted that the sheet, tapers and other paraphernalia of the ceremony had been duly provided by the churchwardens, and the curious in such matters were, of course, on the tip toe of expectation.

'Saturday morning came and towards ten o'clock some hundreds of persons found their way into the Parish Church, where the presence of the curate, the churchwardens, and a proctor from the Consistorial Court, seemed to give colour to the prevailing rumours. A large white cloth, which hung most suspiciously within the vestry door also gave confirmation strong of the reality of the coming ceremony, and the eager sightseers arranged themselves in the most convenient parts of the building to witness it.

'The galleries were filled by a motley assemblage of both sexes, every seat in the vicinity of the communion table was crowded with occupants, and the venerable old structure presented more the appearance of a theatre or cockpit, than of a place of Christian worship. Fortunately for public decorum and decency, all this eager curiousity was doomed to disappointment. About twenty minutes after then the culprit entered the church and proceeded to the vestry room; but there were no bare feet, no white sheet, no lighted tapers, but a simple form of recantation was read over and subscribed to, and the crowd who thronged the sacred edifice, finding there was no fun to be seen, quietly dispersed.'

18 OCTOBER **1928** Colebridge House in Longlevens, once the address of an impecunious aristocrat, occupied the ground where the Double Gloucester pub now stands. In the ebbing years of the nineteenth century the Marquis and Marchioness of Townsend lived a leisurely life in France, accompanied by the Marchioness's lady-in-waiting, Mrs Sullivan.

A former sea captain of Cheltenham served under Nelson.

TOWN HALL, CHELTENHAM,

On Saturday Evening, October 21st, 1905,

Grand Concert

TO CELEBRATE THE

CENTENARY of NELSON'S GREAT VICTORY at TRAFALGAR, 1805.

THE MUSICAL FESTIVAL SOCIETY'S

GRAND CONCERT ON TRAFALGAR DAY.

LORD NELSON.

MISCELLANEOUS PROGRAMME AND TABLEAUX

300 PERFORMERS.

Conductor—Mr. J. A. MATTHEWS.

TICKETS—1/- 2/6 3/- 4/- 6/- at WESTLEY & Co's., THE PROMENADE

The fifth Marquis was a playboy and enjoyed a flutter, which assisted his passage to the bankruptcy court, a destination he reached shortly before his death in 1899. His unfortunate widow now found herself with no husband, home, or means, and in an ironic reversal of roles became dependent on her lifelong servant, Mrs Sullivan.

The pair came to Gloucester and lived in a house a door or two away from the King Edward pub in Longlevens. Then, in about 1911, Colebridge House became available, which Mrs Sullivan thought a more appropriate residence for her titled, but penniless, former employer.

The large house and extensive grounds presented Mrs Sullivan with a hefty financial burden. She survived the Marchioness, by which time Colebridge House had swallowed up all Mrs Sullivan's savings and, as it was mortgaged up to the hilt, left her in abject penury. She died penniless on this day, and Colebridge House was demolished in the 1930s.

19 OCTOBER **1401** The largest memorial brass in the country is said to be found in St James's church, Chipping Campden. Measuring 8ft 9in by 44ft 4in it depicts William Grevel, 'The flower of wool merchants of all England', who died this month. The likeness of his wife, looking suitably pious, shares the brass.

20 OCTOBER A traditional autumn treat in rural Gloucestershire was lamb-tail pie. A red-hot iron was used to sever and cauterise in one go the lamb's tail, which was held in place on a wooden block. When a sufficient number had been lopped in this way, the tails were taken to the farmhouse while still warm and scalded in boiling water one at a time, to make removal of the wool easier. Popped chopped into an ovenproof dish along with carrots, onion and whatever else was to hand, then covered in pastry preferably made from the lard of a newly killed pig, lamb-tail pie was nutritious, though not for the faint-hearted. Another seasonal favourite was backbone pie.

21 OCTOBER **1860** Winchcombe town stocks, which were last used in this year, stand outside the museum on the corner of the High Street and North Street. Count the number of leg holes and you will find there are seven. Was Winchcombe once plagued by a gang of four which included a one-legged villain?

If a gang of seven one-legged villains arrived in town, Winchcombe was prepared.

1976   Until its closure, S.J. Morelands, makers of England's Glory matches, was one of Gloucester's best-known firms. The idea of printing jokes on the back of matchboxes was started by Morelands in the early years of last century. Eventually about 500 different ditties were used a year, each one personally chosen by Sam Moreland who, when once asked how he selected a suitable joke, replied 'If it makes me laugh, we don't use it.' Here's an example. 'A gentleman named Hardwick by a cricket ball was struck. Five words were on his tombstone – Hardwick, hard ball, hard luck.'   22 OCTOBER

1121   Tewkesbury Abbey, consecrated on this date, has many splendid tombs. Among the most curious is the Wakeman cenotaph, which is found at the east end of the church and commemorates the last abbot of Tewkesbury. Carved in stone is the figure of a monk, whose decomposing body is being burrowed into by a worm, slithered on by a snake, jumped on by a frog, nibbled at by a mouse and crawled over by a snail.   23 OCTOBER

Above: Detail of the Wakeman cenotaph.
Left: The Wakeman cenotaph, Tewkesbury Abbey.

'How charming', you may be thinking. But the tomb was intended to tell a story, a story that was interrupted by history. The original idea was that a likeness of Wakeman would be placed at the top of the tomb, with the mouldy old monk beneath it. This would remind mediaeval minds that no matter how rich and prosperous you are in this life, you should not become proud and above yourself because ultimately we are all just skin and bones.

The likeness of Wakeman in his robes and splendour was never added to the monument, because when the Dissolution of the Monasteries came about in 1539, Wakeman left Tewkesbury to become Bishop of Gloucester.

24 OCTOBER Cheltenham's most famous epitaph must be:

> Here lie I and my three daughters.
> Died from drinking Cheltenham waters.
> If we'd stuck to Epsom salts,
> we wouldn't be in these damp vaults.

In fact the rhyme never appeared on any tombstone. The verse was printed in a Bath newspaper at the end of the eighteenth century and was intended as a joke at the expense of the new, upstart spa.

25 OCTOBER **1906** Great excitement was caused in the city on this day when there was a breakout from Gloucester gaol. Five inmates managed to go over the wall unnoticed. Then they ran down to the river and forced a chap named Henry Bubb to row them across to Castle Meadow. They managed to remain at large for some weeks, but were eventually caught by a local Bobby hiding in a haystack at Lydney. So filthy, lousy and hungry were the five that they whistled to attract the constable's attention, for fear he might not discover them.

26 OCTOBER **1941** Swindon villagers preparing to go to church on this day heard a dangerously low-flying aircraft passing overhead. Some looked out of windows to see a Vickers Wellington bomber in serious trouble. The drone of its twin engines gave way to a howl as the stricken aircraft tipped into a fatal dive. Awestruck villagers looked on as parts of the plane's tail broke off, the nose dropped, then sections of the fuselage and the right wing broke away. The bomber hit the ground close to Home Farm, to the west of the allotments at the end of Stantons Drive. All eight members of the crew were killed.

The inquest that followed gave no firm verdict on why the accident had happened, but it was mooted that the emergency dinghy housed in the wing had inflated while the plane was in flight and wrapped itself around the tail, rendering the controls useless.

27 OCTOBER **1971** The Duke of Norfolk, an eighteenth-century resident of Old Spa House (demolished this month), in Lower Westgate Street and three times mayor of Gloucester, was stinking rich. Actually he was stinking and rich. It is said that

ALONE IN COTTAGE WITH A CORPSE

FIVE YEARS FOR YOUTH WHO KILLED HIS FATHER

(From Our Own Correspondent)

TWO men, father and son, shared a small cottage in the heart of Gloucester City until a night last October, when the parent was killed by violence.

For days the son lived on in the cottage, while the body of his father lay decomposing on the stairs, and then he took his bicycle and disappeared.

Hungry and destitute, he walked unconsciously into a country police-station to beg for food, and a few minutes later found himself under arrest for alleged murder.

Brought to trial at the Assizes, he made no attempt to deny the fatal blows, but pleaded that he acted in self-defence when attacked by his father, a powerful, quick-tempered, and violent man.

He was found guilty, not of murder, but manslaughter, and sentenced to five years' penal servitude

STRUGGLE FOR HAMMER

I KNEW I HAD TO KEEP HITTING HIM "

SISTER'S SMILE FROM THE WITNESS-BOX

GREAT crowds outside Gloucester Shire Hall reflected the county's interest in the trial of Ronald George Wells, aged 19, who for a number of years had travelled with his father round the outlying districts selling cheese from a pony trap

Wells, neatly dressed in a pin-striped navy blue suit, pleaded not guilty to the murder of his father, George Wells, aged 60, by striking him on the head with a hammer or some similar instrument.

His mother, who had lived apart from her husband for a long time before the tragedy, was one of the first people in court, and she took a seat immediately behind the dock and as near as possible to her accused son.

Apparently Ronald Wells did not see her as he stepped up from the cells, but he closely studied the jury, which included three women.

This is the story of the tragedy as Mr. St. John Micklethwaite, K.C., unfolded it for the Crown. On Nov. 2 police forced an entrance to the cottage in St. Mary's-square where accused lived with his

The defence opened with evidence by prisoner himself. He seemed to be agitated, and toyed with his clothing.

On Monday, Oct. 23, he began, he went home at 10.45 p.m., and his father complained of his late hours and drinking. As he sat down his father went to the cellar, and, returning with a shovel of coal, started shouting at him again.

Counsel: Were you drunk?—Wells: No; I had had some beer.

Wells went on to say that as he was unlacing his boots he looked up and saw his father with a hammer raised above his head. Deceased shouted, "I'll teach you to come home like this. You won't go out again."

"I jumped up," said Wells, "forced him back towards his armchair, and caught hold of the hammer. We struggled and I wrenched it from him.

"I was nervous, and knew he was going to hit me in that mood. He caught hold of me again, and I realised I had to keep hitting him to keep him away.

"I hit him and lost my head. The next thing I knew he was lying on the ground. I lifted him up and put him in his armchair. He was heavy, but I managed it.

"I sat down for a while and then washed my hands and face. Blood was all over me. I could not do anything for my father, so I sat in the chair all night.

"I woke up out of a doze at 5 o'clock the next morning and knew he was dead."

Wells explained that he did not say anything of the tragedy to anyone "because he wanted time to think things out," though he went half-way to the police-station several times, but fear

This cutting from the *Citizen* tells the sorry tale of a son who killed his father on 23 October 1934.

he detested soap and water so much that his servants used to wait until he had passed out after a drinking binge, then set to work on him with the carbolic.

The niffy noble once told politician Dudley North he had tried everything to cure his rheumatism, to which North replied, 'But pray my lord, have you ever tried a clean shirt?'

28 OCTOBER 1851 'A Lecture on "Bloomerism" was delivered at the Assembly Rooms, Cheltenham. The lecturer, a Mrs Warrinor, announced her intention of appealing to the "wives, mothers and daughters of England, in favour of Bloomerism, or modern dress reform". She appeared on the platform in full Bloomer costume, but so unpopular was the spectacle that it was received with jeers and titters, and the majority of the audience left the room.' (*Norman's History of Cheltenham*, John Goding, 1863)

29 OCTOBER Parts of Newnham-on-Severn's handsome Victoria Hotel date back to the mid-sixteenth century, though the majority of the building is later. It is said to be haunted by a chambermaid who hanged herself in an attic room.

30 OCTOBER 1893 In the latter years of Victoria's reign, William Hunt Yarnton Mills, son of the Rector of Miserden, was appointed Executive Engineer of Public Works by the Nizam of Hyderabad. Unfortunately he had little time to exult in this prestigious post, as he contracted cholera and died on this day shortly after his arrival in the sub-continent.

31 OCTOBER 1479 George, Duke of Clarence, younger brother of Edward IV, drowned in a vat of Malmsey wine at the age of 28 and was buried at Tewkesbury.

November

✝

Two snippets from the Cheltenham Examiner set our scene for November, the month of shortening days and the onset of winter's worst. On 15 November 1859 Mr Jon Goulder, aged 84, and Mr Samuel Page, 82, well known inhabitants of the town, shot a pigeon match at five birds each, the junior youth being declared the winner. It may be interesting to state that both these sportsmen are town born. Goulder was born at the Eight Bells and was for many years stud groom to the Duke of Gordon, from whom he received as a present the gun which did him such good service in the above match. His opponent Page served under the immortal Nelson and was present at the cutting out of the French flotilla in Boulogne Harbour in 1801. Less than a week earlier on 9 November 1859 Mr G.T.F. Smith died. He was well known in Cheltenham for prophesying the state of the weather, and foretelling individual and national destinies from planetary influences. He was a great sufferer from asthma, and his death occurred at the age of 65.

1 NOVEMBER   **1834**   Until its removal in the 1970s a tombstone in Cheltenham Parish church commemorated a woman with an unbeatably concise surname. Mary Wooley H died in this year.

2 NOVEMBER   **1784**   Tom, Dick and Harry, three brothers with the surname Dunston, were Gloucestershire's most notorious highwaymen. They were in business during the latter half of the eighteenth century and plied their trade in Wychwood Forest, near Stow-on-the-Wold. The trio rose to infamy by holding up the Gloucester-to-Oxford stagecoach, a heist that bagged them hundreds of pounds. But less lucky was their attempt to burgle Tangley Manor, between Stow and Burford. The household had been tipped off and laid a trap. When Dick put his hand through the grill in the front door to unlatch the lock, his arm was noosed and held fast. Rather than allow himself to be caught, Dick commanded his brothers to lop his arm off, which they did.

Not surprisingly, Dick gave up highway robbery after this mishap, though his brothers continued in the thieving business until this year, when they unsuccessfully tried to shoot the landlord of an inn. The bullet bounced off the innkeeper's money belt, saving his life and, in the commotion that followed, the local constabulary arrived and apprehended Tom and Harry, who were hanged in Gloucester gaol at dawn on this dank November day.

3 NOVEMBER   **1939**   Major G.C.W. Willis, ARP officer in charge, issued this stern rebuke to the people of Gloucester: 'The number of active wardens in the city barely reaches the authorised establishment, and allows absolutely no reserves at all. It's not fair that the majority should leave it to the few to do their duty.

'If one man does his work all day at the factory and then is prepared to turn out at night and lose his sleep while on duty, every able bodied man should be prepared to do the same.'

In the following week's *Gloucester Journal* Major Willis's red-with-rage face was replaced by egg-on-face farce when it was revealed that plenty of people had offered their services as wardens, but the ARP had lost their application forms.

4 NOVEMBER   **1697**   Katherine Gardiner of Bibury found herself on the receiving end of rough justice, seventeenth-century style, when she was compelled to undergo the public humiliation of standing in the churchyard 'barefooted, barelegged and bareheaded having a white sheet over her wearing apparell and holding a white rod in her hand, then go into the church and confess to the gathered congregation her fornication, having been delivered of a bastard child'.

5 NOVEMBER   **1876**   Bonfire night has long been an excuse for high jinks, as this report from the *Tewkesbury Examiner* reminds us. 'Groups of young fellows furnished with nipple canons [?] paraded the streets and discharged the canons against a lamp post with deafening noise. A large mob at the Cross pelted passers with squibs, crackers and other flaming missiles which caused horses to be frightened. Shortly after 9pm the gig house near the old eagle factory was a mass of flame and was destroyed with its contents.'

1825 In Norman's *History of Cheltenham*, published in 1863, appears a list of long-lived inhabitants of the town. Most senior among them is Richard Lily, who at the time of his demise this month was 106. Others who continued to bat on after notching up a century are Mary Lane, died 1815 aged 102, Dinah Chestero, died 1830 aged 103, and Bartholemew Cassidy, who hopped along to the other side in 1862, also aged 103.

Nonagenarians are ten-a-penny, among them the picturesquely named Thomas Clutterbuck, Charlotte Osbaldiston, Anne Blessauxnax and Moses Moses.

Perhaps the most unfortunate was Sarah Bradstock, who died at the age of 105 in 1847, an inmate of the Cheltenham Workhouse, where she had resided for the best part of 50 years.

6 NOVEMBER

Below, left: 'A' list celebrities on the Cheltenham longevity chart. *Below:* The death of long-lived Mrs Bullock is reported.

INSTANCES OF LONGEVITY ATTAINED BY DECEASED INHABITANTS OF CHELTENHAM.

Year of decease.	Name.	Age.	Year of decease.	Name.	Age.
1791	Hannah Leach	96	1846	Elizabeth Little	94
1795	Anne Hopkins	93	1847	Thomas Mason	91
1800	Mary Stevens	92	"	Samuel Davis	96
1803	Anne Andrews	94	"	Sarah Bradstock	105
1815	Ann Angelic	91	"	Mary Gardner	91
"	Mary Lane	102	"	Caroline Tanner	90
"	Richard Sherrington	91	1848	Thomas Walker	91
1825	Richard Lily	106	"	Ann Griffith	91
"	Esther Strond	104	"	Ann Green	92
"	Thomas Williams	102	1849	William Jordan	92
"	Thomas Morgan	91	"	Richard Webb	96
1830	Dinah Chestero	103	"	W. Jordan	90
1833	Sarah Brown	98	"	Elizabeth Champion	90
1835	Eliza Harding	100	"	Elizabeth M. Keating	97
"	Elizabeth Fry	103	"	Elizabeth Pimble	98
1836	Robert Chambers	99	"	Ann C. Douglas	92
1837	Martha Williams	99	"	Jane Rose	94
1839	Mary Betteridge	97	1850	Sarah Kench	90
"	John Brown	99	"	Francis Radnal	93
1840	William Pantin	96	"	Ann Webb	97
1842	Elizabeth Workman	102	"	John West	92
1843	Sarah Kingham	97	"	Elizabeth Morgan	92
"	Sarah Hiam	99	"	Phillipa Shaw	95
"	Thomas Starr	90	1851	Nicholas Allen	90
"	Sarah Wellsman	90	"	William Wilks	91
"	Ann Sweeney	92	1852	Mary Maisey	97
1844	Benjamin Johnson	95	"	Elizabeth Greening	91
"	William Holford	92	"	Elizabeth C. Stephens	91
"	Isabella Rogers	91	"	Rev. Sir R. Wolseley, Bart.	92
1845	Francis Crompton	93	"	Jane Johnstone	94
"	Anne Blessauxnax	91	"	Charlotte Cotton	97
"	Elizabeth Weake	90	1853	Ann Davies	91
"	Mary Smith	90	"	Louisa Cook	96
"	Jane Heming	92	"	Ann Iredell	92
1846	James Hawkins	90	"	Harriett Till	94
"	Mary Page	90	"	Martha Rose	91
"	Anne Lowe	91	"	Charlotte Scott	104
"	Sarah Bagott	90	1854	David Home	91
"	Gilbert Jones	91	"	Elizabeth Cook	97

Death of a Cheltenham Centenarian.
Mrs. Bullock, who died a few days ago at the residence of her daughter, Mrs. Marchant, 6 Gratton-street, Cheltenham, where she had lived for some two years, aged 102 years. She came to Cheltenham as a young woman from Horsley, near Stroud, where she was born, and has lived in St. James's district over 80 years.

1942 P.E.G. Sayer OBE, Gloster Aircraft's chief test pilot, was killed in a flying accident. He was the first man to fly a Gloster Gladiator, which was the last biplane to see active service with the RAF. Sayer was also involved in early testing of the Hurricane, when GAC was taken over by Hawkers. But his place in aviation history is assured, because he piloted the E28/39, Britain's first jet aeroplane, on its maiden flight in May 1941.

7 NOVEMBER

8 NOVEMBER

1886 On this day Frederick Archer, the most celebrated jockey of his time, shot himself through the mouth with his own revolver in the bedroom of his house in Newmarket. Raised in a cottage behind the Kings Arms at Prestbury, Archer was 29 years old at the time of his death. The coroner's verdict was that he had taken his own life while in a state of temporary insanity induced by typhoid fever.

His estate was £66,662, a staggering sum in today's terms. This was bequeathed to his family, with £1,000 to his valet, Solomon. Perhaps the best memorial to this remarkable sportsman rests in the statistics of his career: 8,004 mounts, 2,148 wins.

Champion jockey took his own life.

THE LATE FRED ARCHER,
the famous jockey; a native of Cheltenham, and son of the lady whose death has just taken place. With him is his young wife, who died in 1884, about eighteen months after their marriage.

9 NOVEMBER

1854 This reminder that a splendid name is no protection against rough justice appeared in the *Gloucestershire Chronicle*: 'Cornelius Clutterbuck, an idle urchin, was brought up before the court charged with stealing apples from an enclosed orchard at Arle. With the consent of the prosecutor, the magistrate, Mr. Pilkington, said he would discharge the lad on the promise that he should be well flogged by his father.'

10 NOVEMBER

Kings John's Bridge, Tewkesbury.

1038 King John's bridge has straddled the Avon at Tewkesbury for some 800 years. The original early thirteenth-century bridge built on the orders of the monarch was of stone, with a half-mile-long wooden causeway across the Ham. To ensure that the bridge was well maintained, King John declared that tolls from Tewkesbury markets on Wednesdays and Saturdays should be earmarked for its upkeep. This did not happen, however, and at the County Assizes in 1638 Tewkesbury was instructed to repair the bridge because 'diverse of his majesty's subjects travelling that way have been unfortunately drowned'.

1918 When Great War guns fell silent after the armistice was signed on this day, almost every parish in the country set about raising a plaque to local heroes who had not returned. Bishops Cleeve was one of the first villages in Gloucestershire to raise a stone cross to the fallen, which was unveiled in September 1919.

1931 'Splintered timber and iron bars were thrown into the air as the racing engines crashed through the gates and passengers ran to the carriage windows.' That is how the scene was described when *The Devonian*, a famous train of the LMS railway, burst the barriers of California Crossing, Gloucester, in November 1931.

The crossing stood diagonally opposite the war memorial in the Park, just a short distance from Gloucester Eastgate station. Keeper of the crossing was Mr Carpenter, who was about to open the gates to allow *The Devonian* to pass when he heard and saw the double-header (i.e. pulled by two locomotives) express bearing down on him. Seeing the way barred, the engine driver rammed on the brakes, but sheer velocity carried the train onwards, the steel of its locked wheels screaming along the tracks. Mr Carpenter wrestled manfully with the gates until the last moment, then threw himself aside, sustaining cuts and bruises by doing so, as *The Devonian* swept through. Remarkably, the only other party to suffer minor injuries was a horse that had just passed over the crossing and bolted in fear.

1856 *Cheltenham Examiner*. 'Extraordinary hurricane in Cheltenham. About 5 o'clock in the evening the gathering clouds gave indications of an approaching storm. Suddenly, it appeared as though the floodgates of the heavens had been opened and the rain descended, not in drops, but as though poured bodily out of some reservoir above. The storm was accompanied by terrific peals of thunder and gusts of wind which seemed to blow from all parts of the compass at once. The streets were speedily flooded, water traps and drain pipes refused for a time their salutary offices, cellars became full, house tops were saturated, and roofs penetrated, while the spouting of ordinary dwellings bubbled and gurgled under the pressure of the unusual flow.

'In the midst of this terrific downpour, a hurricane swept over a part of the town, committing an amount of devastation which must have been seen to have been believed. Commencing at the Workhouse garden it swept over a tract of ground about 50 yards wide, sweeping away everything movable and prostrating everything permanent which stood in its way. In the Plough gardens pigstyes were unroofed, walls prostrated and in an instant garden frames sent flying through the air, chimneys blown down, and trees in every stage of growth laid prostrate on the ground.

'Passing from thence, the storm swept through the wood of Mr. L. Griffiths, of Marle Hill, making a clean breach among the trees, which large and small were thrown down in the course of a few minutes. In one place a cumbrous wooden house was overturned bodily and one of its windows carried spinning through the air a distance of 300 yards. At another spot a garden wall was laid flat along its entire length and a slaughter house of Mr. Warner completely dismantled, Mr. Warner's two sons having a narrow escape.

But it was in Mr. Griffiths's wood that the storm appears to have reached the climax of its fury; trees were blown down in every direction, large limbs were sent careering through the air as though they were mere wisps of straw, while one stately elm, the monarch of the grove – measuring 70ft in length, 25ft across the roots and 18ft in circumference of the trunk – was overturned as completely as the young saplings by which is was surrounded.'

14 NOVEMBER   **1853**   Fatal accident to Mr Croome, a gentleman of large property, residing at Painswick. The deceased was thrown out of his gig, and had his skull so badly fractured that he died in a few hours.

15 NOVEMBER   **1851**   The pitiable story of an infant named James Clifford was reported in *The Times*. When the young James suffered serious burns at his home in Northwood Green, his father, a labouring man who eschewed doctors, carried the boy two miles to a one-legged spell-caster named Mrs Hampton, who applied a potion of her own composition to the injuries while incanting a charm. The boy died.

At the inquest the jury learnt that young James had died of exhaustion, neglect and improper treatment, but that his parents' actions did not amount to a criminal act.

16 NOVEMBER   **1327**   On this day Edward II was captured, taken to Berkeley castle and cast into a hole in the ground, or an 'oublier', as such places were called in the fourteenth century.

The New Inn, Gloucester, was built to provide accommodation for pilgrims who came to visit Edward II's tomb at the cathedral.

For some weeks Edward was left in the pitch black darkness to paddle about in his own filth and endure the damp, freezing conditions. Then he was murdered by his captors in a grossly unpleasant manner. (For details see the entry for 10 October).

Edward's body was brought to Gloucester and his tomb on the north side of the cathedral's choir became such an attraction for pilgrims that the New Inn, Northgate Street, and other city hostelries were built to provide accommodation. This brought a good deal of trade to Gloucester, so the King's misfortune was the city's gain.

17 NOVEMBER

1851 A lively incident was described by the *Cheltenham Examiner* when a carriage conveying Mrs Erskine of Forthampton tipped over in the High Street. 'The accident is worth recording for the extraordinary career of the runaway horse, who with the shafts dangling behind him, continued to plunge until he had broken the carriage in pieces. He then darted off along Clarence Street with the shafts and fore wheels dangling. On arriving at the end of Clarence Street he turned into the Promenade, where he charged at full gallop the handsome plate glass front of Debenham and Freebody, one of the large panes of which was shivered into a thousand fragments. He then crossed the Promenade onto the pavement on the opposite side, along which he proceeded as far as Imperial Square, and passing along the bottom of the square and down Rodney Terrace, he again reached the High Street, down which he went at the same fearful pace.

'On arriving at the corner of Clarence Street, where he originally started from, he took the narrow passage leading to the Eight Bells, then along the lane by the churchyard wall and through the archway by the Examiner office, again emerging into Imperial Circus. Here he made a second dash at the shop of Messrs. Debenham, but being headed, turned to the right down the

Colonnade and again into the High Street. This time he took the turn up the street towards the Plough Hotel, still showing the same partiality to the pavement, along which he galloped, passing under the portico of the George Hotel, and under the window blinds of several of the shops, until he reached the more open part of the street near the Belle Vue Hotel, where he was captured.'

18 NOVEMBER

A stone obelisk found in the churchyard at Bisley is called the Old Bone House. There are seats carved at the base of its decorative arches, but it is not perhaps a place that many people would choose to sit, relax and watch the world go by. This conical structure marks the spot of the village bone hole,

Bisley Bone House hides a grave secret.

which in times gone by received unidentified bits of human remains that were dug up when gravediggers were going about their work. According to a local legend, in the dim and distant past the village priest was shuffling round the churchyard when, being uncertain of foot, he slipped, fell into the bone hole and died.

When news of this mishap reached the Vatican, the Pope was greatly upset and commanded that no burials take place in Bisley for two years. So for the next twenty-four months funeral cortèges had to wind their way to Bibury, which is about twelve miles away. This is a story difficult to believe, you might quite reasonably think. But to this day there is a part of Bibury graveyard that is called Bisley Piece.

19 NOVEMBER   **1680**   On this day in 1680 William Prynne, a lawyer of Cheltenham, died and was buried in the Parish churchyard. A Protestant extremist, Prynne wrote 'our English gentlewomen are now grown so far past shame as to clip their hair like men and make this whorish cut the fashion of the times'.

Besides complaining about women's hairdos, he published a book titled *Histriomastrix*, which was declared blasphemous and subversive. In punishment, Prynne was barred from the bar, fined £5,000, placed in the pillory at Cheapside and again at Westminster, had both his ears cut off and was imprisoned in the Tower of London, where he set about writing another book on the same theme.

This time he was fined another £5,000, placed in the pillory once more, ordered to have his ears cut off a second time, branded, and cast into the dungeon of Caernarvon castle. With the Restoration in 1649 he was set free, married a girl from Cirencester (whom we may suppose sported long, flowing locks) and moved to Cheltenham.

20 NOVEMBER   The Priory church at Deerhurst is a fine example of Saxon architecture. In the floor of the north aisle is a brass measuring 7ft 5in by 3ft to Sir John Cassy

Deerhurst dog brass is unique.

and his wife. At the feet of Lady Cassy is a dog labelled Terri. This is the only example of a monumental brass in England that shows a named pet.

In times of yore, villagers at Bourton-on-the-Water believed that a live pigeon placed under the bed of a dying person would prolong the life of the occupant.

21 NOVEMBER

1861 *Cheltenham Examiner*. 'Died, at Beaufort Villas, Major-General Derinzey. He went through the Peninsular campaigns, was severely wounded through both knees at Corunna, was run through the body and left for dead at the Battle of Neville; he was twice wounded, musket ball in the left arm, and by a splinter of a shell in the chest, at the Battle of Toulouse, but did not quit the field.'

22 NOVEMBER

Behind the Greenway Hotel at Shurdington stands an oak tree of impressive girth and venerable age. According to local lore, three sheep stealers were hanged from its boughs in the eighteenth century after a cursory, country-style trial.

23 NOVEMBER

Funerals rarely took place on a Monday in the Forest of Dean. Foresters believed that if a grave were dug on a Saturday and left open on a Sunday the Devil would lie there in wait for the soul of the deceased.

24 NOVEMBER

Monday was a no-no for Forest funerals. This photograph shows the Devil's Chapel, Forest of Dean. *(Martin Latham)*

25 NOVEMBER   **1753**   Anne Williams became the last woman to be burned at the stake in Gloucester. She had been found guilty of poisoning her husband.

26 NOVEMBER   **1845**   *Cheltenham Examiner*: 'Died at his residence, Cheltenham, aged 67, Admiral Sir Salisbury Davenport KCB, KCH. The deceased officer, who took the name of Davenport on his marriage with a heiress of that name, was the Captain Humphreys who on 22 June 1807, when in command of the Leopard fifty gun frigate, captured the American frigate Chesapeake on the Halifax station. The action took place under written instructions from the late Admiral Sir George Berkeley, ordering the Leopard to search any American vessels he might fall in with, for deserters from the English navy. He demanded to search the Chesapeake, which her captain refused to permit: he thereupon engaged the American, killing six and wounding 22 of her crew. After the Chesapeake had struck her colours five British seamen were found aboard her, and on their being brought to trial as deserters one was hanged, and the others sentenced to 500 lashes each.'

27 NOVEMBER   A row of cottages, once quaintly named Ship's Yud Row, can be found in Littledean. They look onto a lane where a pair of impressively dressed ghosts are seen to swagger from time to time. The sartorially splendid spectral figures are said to be Royalist Cavalier soldiers who were killed in a scuffle with Parliamentarians during the Civil War.

28 NOVEMBER   **1857**   The news was reported of a 'Distressing accident in the hunting field to Mrs. E. Dangerfield, of 1, Berkeley Villas, Gloucester. Mrs. Dangerfield was riding on her pony when the horse of one of the field struck out with tremendous force, inflicting a compound fracture of the bones of the leg. The "gentleman?" riding the vicious brute galloped on without stopping to enquire into the extent of the injury.'

29 NOVEMBER   **1787**   Some of the yew trees in the churchyard of St Mary's, Painswick, are shaped like field mushrooms, others are plump and rounded like freshly baked bloomers. There are cones and orbs, upright box-shapes and dumpy bap-like trees, but most importantly, there are ninety-nine.

Most of the cleverly clipped trees were saplings in 1800. And according to local lore it is impossible to round their number up to 100. Every time one is planted, another dies, so the churchyard remains, like a nervous batsman, forever one short of its century. Some say this incomplete number is the work of the Devil, but Laurie Lee suggested a different kind of devilment. According to the author of *Cider with Rosie* it was because people from his village of Slad dug up a tree at dead of night each time a new one was planted, just to irk the posh folk of Painswick.

Another feature of the churchyard is its ornate table and pedestal tombs. Embellished with skulls, bones and other reminders of mortality, these are mostly the work of local stonemason John Bryan, who died on this day in 1787 and is buried in the churchyard beneath a stone pyramid.

Painswick tombs are
the work of local
stonemason John
Bryan.

John Bryan's pyramid
tomb, Painswick.

30 NOVEMBER **1843** When fire broke out at a farmhouse at Willesley, Broadway, on this November night, the occupant Mrs Rimel and six of her children perished in the flames.

NOVEMBER **1938** In November of this year Billy Thomas and his Gloucester Accordion Band played a dinner dance at the refurbished New Hotel in Southgate Street. Tickets were priced at *7s 6d*. For anyone who enjoyed the sound of eight accordions being played simultaneously in a confined space, this must have been a joy.

DECEMBER

✠

Many people have heard of the rhyme that was once found on a tombstone in St Mary's churchyard, Cheltenham:

To the memory of John Higgs, died 1825.

Here lies John Higgs
A famous man for killing pigs,
For killing pigs was his delight
Both morning, afternoon and night.
Both heats and cold he did endure,
Which no physician could e're cure.
His knife is laid, his work is done,
I hope to heaven his soul is gone.

Perhaps less well known is the curious fact that John Higgs' descendant Albert, who lived in Hesters Way Cottage, Hesters Way Lane, was commissioned to make a coffin for a dog named Toddy. This was the pet of Natalia Owens, the daughter of a Lieutenant Colonel in the Somerset Light Infantry.
Sad though it is to report, Christmas was not a time of festive merriment for Lady Pynn of Cheltenham, or Lettie Davies of Gloucester. As you will read, her ladyship met an unfortunate end when her nightie went up in flames, while Ms Davies celebrated the season so freely that she had to be wheeled to the nick in a sack truck.

1 December **1934** The *Citizen's* lead story in 1934 told the tale of a particularly gruesome murder. This concerned a 19-year-old man who returned home to 48 St Mary's Square and became involved in an argument with his father. Harsh words gave way to violence, and the son battered his father's head with a hammer until he was dead.

The father and son were well known about the city and outlying parts, as they ran a business selling cheese from a pony and trap. For two weeks after the tragic event the son continued to live in the cottage with his father's body slumped on the stairway. When neighbours and customers asked where the old man was, the son made excuses. Then the 19-year-old disappeared too. Police were summoned and broke into the house where they found the blood stained corpse. A warrant for the arrest of the son was put out and he was soon apprehended. The young man had cycled to South Wales, where he had gone to a police station and asked for food, as he had no money. He was found guilty of manslaughter and sentenced to five years.

2 December Theatrical groups around the county at this time of year are in final rehearsals for their annual pantomime, and many will no doubt be staging the story of Dick Whittington and his cat. R. Whittington Esq. was a local chap. According to tradition he came from Coberley, and effigies of his parents can be seen in the village church.

He really was Lord Mayor of London three times – in 1397, 1406 and 1419 – and he really did leave his country home to seek his fortune in the capital; very successfully too. He was a cloth merchant and became so wealthy he loaned large sums to the king.

All of that is true, but – alas – the story of his cat is not. When Lord Mayor, Whittington had his portrait painted in his ceremonial robes. In the tradition of the time, the artist captured Dick holding a skull as a symbol of mortality. Centuries later, by which time the fashion for skulls had passed, an art dealer came into possession of the picture and painted out the bony cranium, replacing it with a moggy in the belief that it would make the portrait easier to sell.

3 December **1883** A local newspaper advertisement commends Liebig's Chemical Food. 'A nutritious and invigorating essence highly recommended by the most eminent of the medical profession for the cure of nervous head and mind complaints, coughs, asthma and incipient consumption, nervousness, weakness and exhaustion; dimness of sight, shortness of breath; headache, depression, palpitation of the heart; drowsiness, indigestion; singing noises in the ears, trembling, loss of memory; want of appetite, neuralgia pains and aches; wasting disorders, loss of energy, impaired nutrition, inactivity of the brain, dullness of perception and delusions – which if not attended to in time – may become serious.'

4 December **1861** *Cheltenham Examiner*. 'Death of Thomas Pilkington Esq., Chairman of the Bench Magistrates. We feel, while making this announcement, that it affords the subject for more posthumous eulogy. During a residence of more than a quarter of a century in Cheltenham Mr. Pilkington has endeared himself to the hearts of thousands amongst us by the force of his character, the integrity of his principles, by the kindness of his disposition, by his conduct as a magistrate and private citizen, and by unnumbered acts of private and public munificence. Of his loss it may truly be said that 'Take him for all in all, We ne're shall look upon his like again' and the public funeral, which is this day accorded to his remains, will be no mere idle pageant, but the 'outward and visibly sign' of that deep sorrow at his loss which pervades the hearts of every class of his fellow-townsmen.'

5 December

1946 Charles Trigg, known as Hell for Leather Charlie, was the country's leading flat-racing jockey in his day. Born at Minsterworth, he rode 111 winners in 1911, and during his career was first pass the post of every major race on the calendar: the Chester Cup, Cesarewitch, the Oaks, Goodwood Cup, Lincoln Handicap and Royal Hunt Cup – Charlie won them all. He also rode Edward VII's horse to victory at Sandown Park.

Despite a glittering career in Britain, France, Austria and Eire, Charlie Trigg ended his days in poverty and obscurity, reduced to one-room lodgings in St Mary's Street, Gloucester. He died on this day at the age of 65.

Hell for Leather Charlie was top jockey in his day.

6 December

1704 The church of St John at Elkstone has the distinction of standing on higher ground than any other in the Cotswolds. It is also notable for its intact registers, which date back to 1592. Some especially quirky entries were made by William Prior, who was Rector from 1682 to 1725. One such is '6th December 1704 was buried the stinking residue of William Gwylliams'.

1143 Milo Fitzwater, the founder of St Briavels Castle in the Forest of Dean, was killed while hunting in 1143 by an arrow that rebounded off a tree.

7 December

1760 Bill Clavers, the landlord of the Ragged Cot Inn at Hyde, near Minchinhampton, robbed the night coach to London. Having partaken of much Dutch courage, he was about to set off into the night with his loaded pistols when his wife, who was great with child, tried to prevent him and was pushed down the stair for her pains.

On his return with the ill-gotten gains, Clavers found his wife and newborn child dead, and bundled both into a trunk. Constables soon arrived at the Ragged Cot, having followed Clavers' footprints in the snow. He fired at them but gave himself up when the spectral figures of his wife and child appeared. Clavers was hanged at Gloucester.

9 DECEMBER   **1854**   The 'Death under most distressing circumstances' was reported of Mrs Daniel Alder, of Imperial Circus, Cheltenham. 'Mrs. Alder was a lady well known and respected, her husband had been honourably known for 40 years, yet while his wife was lying dead in the house, and himself, to all appearance, on the point of death, his creditors forced him into the Bankruptcy Court, a proceeding which evoked an amount of sympathy on behalf of the family such as is rarely witnessed.'

10 DECEMBER   **1902**   Above Dog Kennel Wood on the lower slopes of Leckhampton Hill is a cairn of limestone blocks, no doubt hewn from Leckhampton Quarry, surrounded by the remains of an iron fence. Carved into the face of the stone that tops the pile are these words:

Cairn recalls favourite horse.

To the memory of The Continental,
by Boulevarde – Fairhaven, foaled 1891. Died 1902.
Winner of twenty-five steeplechases,
and the favourite hunter of Cecil Elwes,
by whom these stones were erected.

The unfortunate horse caught its leg in farm equipment while being exercised and severed a vein, causing so great a loss of blood that the animal had to be put down.

1940   On this day at 7.20 p.m. the Luftwaffe dropped siting flares over Cheltenham, and ten minutes later incendiary, high-explosive and oil bombs fell – over 100 in total. One smashed through the roof of a house in Pilley Crescent, Leckhampton, and became embedded in the kitchen floor without going off. Other bombs landed at Southfield Farm in nearby Church Road, in Burrows playing-field and the allotments in Hall Road, adjacent to Leckhampton primary school. The railway bridge in Shurdington Road was narrowly missed. H.H. Martyn's Sunningend factory was hit and set ablaze, which served to direct other Luftwaffe raiders to the scene. Half Stoneville Street was demolished when a large bomb landed on the railway embankment nearby, killing ten people, some of them children. On the other side of Gloucester Road a gas holder was hit, as was Parkwood Mansion flats in Shurdington Road, where five residents died. In addition to these fatalities 600 people in the town were made homeless.

11 December

1874   Gloucestershire shepherds were regarded as being among the most skilled of their kind, because of the county's long history of sheep-rearing. During the nineteenth century many local shepherds were lured to Australia

12 December

Cotswold shepherds sailed into oblivion.

and New Zealand by the promise of better wages, working conditions and a more clement climate. For some the adventure was the making of them, which is why so many families from down under trace their roots back to this part of the world. But on others fate smiled less kindly. On the village green at Shipton-under-Wychwood is a fountain that commemorates seventeen local men who sailed with hundreds of other would-be immigrants to New Zealand this year. En route the ship caught fire, and of the 500 on board, just three survived.

13 DECEMBER   **1892**   Now in the keeping of Gloucester Folk Museum is a 3-in square of lead which was discovered in a cupboard beside the chimney of a house called Wilton Place, Dymock, in 1892. Scratched onto the surface are symbols of the occult, magic numbers and esoteric runes, all of which were intended to place a curse on a local lass named Sarah Ellis. The wording, some of it inscribed backwards, reads 'Hasmodat, Acteus, Magalesius, Ormenus, Lieus, Nicon, Mimon, Zeper, Make this person to Banish away from this place and Countery Amen. To my desier Amen.'

Who Sarah Ellis was and what she did to attract such a curse we will never know. But curiously, just two miles outside Dymock is a spot on the parish boundary that was once widely known as Ellis Cross. The name was taken from a person who committed suicide and, in keeping with seventeenth-century tradition, was buried at the nearest crossroads with a wooden stake driven through the heart.

14 DECEMBER   **1862**   On this day was reported a 'Fatal accident to Mr. Stewart Thompson at Andoversford while out with the Cotswold hounds. The horse fell and threw his rider, inflicting at the same time, a kick to the back part of the head, which fractured the base of his skull.'

15 DECEMBER   **1855**   *Cheltenham Examiner*: 'Lieut. Battine, his brother, and two other officers of Chatham garrison, drowned by the upsetting of a boat on the river Medway. The young Battines were intimately known in Cheltenham, where their late father, General Battine, resided, and where, indeed, their widowed mother, as well as many near and dear relatives still live. The painful bereavement to which Mrs. Battine has thus been subjected, was most feelingly alluded to by the Rev. A. Boyd in the course of his sermon at Christ Church on the following Sunday morning'.

16 DECEMBER   **1294**   Gloucestershire's only heart burial can be found in Coberley church. The removed organ once beat inside the body of Sir Giles Berkeley, who endured the rigours of fighting in the Crusades, only to return home and die from illness in Malvern this year.

It was the norm for crusader knights slain in far-flung and hot parts to have their heart sent home for interment, as transporting a complete dead body before the invention of refrigeration was no easy matter. However, conveying a corpse from Malvern to Coberley would not have been too taxing even without cold storage facilities, so we must assume Sir Giles thought that as other crusaders ended their days with bits of them in various places, he would too.

1892   St Peter's, Winchcombe, boasts some of the most grotesque gargoyles in the Cotswolds. There are forty of them in total, some representing demons, ghouls and ghastlies, while the remainder are caricatures of people who lived thereabouts at the time the waterspouts were carved.

17 DECEMBER

In the nave are two stone coffins discovered when the site of the Benedictine abbey was excavated by archaeologists in 1892. One is said to contain the remains of St Kenelm, the boy saint. The other is that of King Kenulf, who ruled the Saxon Kingdom of Mercia from 796 to 821.

When Kenelm became the boy King of Mercia in 819, his jealous sister Quendryda plotted to do away with him and take the crown for herself. She paid Kenelm's guardian Askobert to cut off the young monarch's head in a wood, whereupon his spirit assumed the guise of a dove and flew to Rome. There the dove presented details of the evil doings to the Pope. His holiness despatched investigators to look into the matter, who were helped in their work by the people of Gloucestershire, who pointed the finger at the dead King's sister.

Angered by their cooperation Quendryda attempted to put a curse on local people by reciting the 108th Psalm backwards, but while doing so her eyeballs fell out, splattering blood about the place. She then died, and as no churchyard would accept her body for burial, it was thrown into a ditch and left to rot. Kenelm's body was taken to Winchcombe and interred.

Winchcombe gargoyles.

18 December **1732** Eli Hatton was the last man to be hanged in chains from the gibbet on Pingery Tump, near Mitcheldean. After his execution for murder in 1732, Hatton's body was left in public view. Eventually it reached such a stage of decomposition that traders in Mitcheldean market protested that flies from the corpse were tainting their meat. The corpse was removed.

19 December **1965** Ploddy Farm lies between Newent and Huntley. In days gone by, robbers broke in and killed all members of the household, except for a serving-maid who hid in a barn. The robbers' dog found the hiding maid, took a shine to the girl and remained with her when its wicked masters left. When a posse of locals was raised to find the miscreants, they let the dog go and it led them to the robbers, who were sharing their booty in the pub at Over, where they were promptly lynched. (Information taken from the *Gloucester Journal* of this date.)

20 December **1860** On this day in 1860 was reported the 'Death of George Russell Esq., High Bailiff of Cheltenham. There are few public officers who have commanded so general an amount of respect, and maintained for so many years such a universal popularity as the late High Bailiff of Cheltenham. His genial disposition and good temper, his integrity and impartiality in the discharge of difficult duties, and in mediating between different interests, formed, no doubt, the secret of this popularity and respect. By his death the town loses a good public officer, and his loss will be mourned by a large circle of warm and attached friends. The deceased gentleman was 62 years of age and of this term of existence nearly forty years were spent in the service of the public.'

21 December **1817** In the days when a resident pauper meant a rise in the parish rates, locals were often keen to see vagrants on their way, as this report from the *Gloucester Journal* reminds us. 'On the morning of Saturday a poor weather beaten mariner was discovered lying in a ditch into which he had fallen in the parish of Sandhurst, in the vicinity of this city, and was extricated from his perilous situation, in almost a lifeless state, by a gentleman who accidentally saw him, and by whom he was placed under the care of some persons who undertook to send for the overseer of the poor.

'Towards the close of the day, however, the poor fellow had crawled so far as the Leigh, about midway between this city and Tewkesbury, the overseers of which place put him into a stable, where they suffered him to remain all night with only a little hay to lie on and a single blanket to cover him. On the Sunday morning he was informed that he must proceed on his journey, notwithstanding he earnestly entreated to be suffered to remain there and die. After proceeding a little way, he was unable to walk further, when the overseers procured a horse and conveyed him to Tewkesbury, where he arrived in a most debilitated state. The overseers of that borough, though he was brought in so illegal a manner and during the time of Divine Service on Sunday, perceiving his helpless and miserable condition, ordered him to be immediately conveyed to the house of industry, where proper medical aid and every comfort which that well regulated establishment afforded, was administered with promptitude and where he now lies with very little hopes of recovery.

'The unfortunate man's name is Ellis Francis, a native of Clynnog, near Caernarvon, where his mother now resides on a small farm and for which place he was now proceeding after many years of absence at sea. He was wrecked off the island of Madeira on 26th February last, in the *Rebecca* under Captain Pricknipple on his voyage from Jamaica to Liverpool, when the whole of the crew were drowned expect himself, the captain and mate who remained together on a raft eight and forty hours and were then picked up by a Falmouth packet and conveyed to port where his fellow sufferers soon after died'.

1348 *The Black Death.* An outbreak of bubonic plague that originated in China, reached England in 1348. So virulent was the visitation that it wiped out one third of the total population of the country. Many rural settlements disappeared altogether, including 200 in Gloucestershire.

22 December

1756 The churchwarden's end-of-year accounts for Swindon Village include the following entries: '1756. To George Fluck for making stocks 5/11d'. '1757. To a whipping post and stocks 9/6d'. '1795. Paid for tea, sugar and rise when the poor had the smallpox 14/5d'. And more mysteriously '1774. To Charles Hawker for mending ye town pishe ax 1/4d'.

23 December

1849 On Christmas Eve Lady Pynn was burned to death at her residence in Cheltenham's Promenade. Convalescing after a long illness, she was dozing by her drawing-room fire, when a stray spark spat from the hearth and ignited her muslin nightie. Her ladyship was so shockingly burned that death ensued in a few hours.

24 December

Fire fighters were unable to save Lady Pynn.

25 December **1883** From the *Gloucester Journal*: 'Lettie Davies, a decrepit old woman, was charged with being drunk and incapable. PC Barting found the prisoner lying on the pavement in such a state of drink that he had to remove her to the station in a sack truck.'

BY ROYAL AUTHORITY 1838—1885—1901—1911.

JOHN DOBELL & CO. LTD.,
Importers and Wholesale Dealers
in Wines and Spirits,
CHELTENHAM, TEWKESBURY, AND NEWPORT.

The following Wines and Spirits may be procured (for Cash only) at any of Messrs. Dobell's Branch Establishments:—

SPIRITS. (BY IMPERIAL MEASURE.)

	Per Gal.	Per Pint.	Per ½-Pt.	Per ¼-Pt.	Per Bot.
BRANDY—FINEST BRITISH	20/-	2/6	1/3	-/7½	3/6
GOOD FRENCH, PALE OR BROWN	23/-	3/-	1/6	-/9	4/-
FINEST SELECTED OLD, superior to ordinary } Case Brandy—PALE	29/-	3/9	1/11	1/-	5/-
BROWN	29/-	3/9	1/11	1/-	5/-
GINGER	16/-	2/-	1/-	-/6	2/10
HENNESSY'S *** BRANDY, 6 3 per bottle ; 3/4 per ½-bottle					
RUM—FINE STRONG	18/-	2/4	1/2	-/7	3/2
OLD JAMAICA	21/-	2/8	1/4	-/8	3/6
WHISKEY—GOOD IRISH (strength between 30 and 40 U.P)	17/4	2/2	1/1	-/6½	3/-
BEST IRISH	20/-	2/6	1/3	-/8	3/6
SPECIAL BLEND SCOTCH (strength between } 30 and 10 U.P.)	17/4	2/2	1/1	-/6½	3/-
EXTRA QUALITY BLEND SCOTCH	20/-	2/6	1/3	-/8	3/6
OLD LOCHNAGAR	23/-	3/-	1/6	-/9	4/-
JOHNNIE WALKER'S, DEWAR'S, and BUCHANAN'S WHISKIES 4/- per bottle ; 2/1 per ½-bottle					
GIN—FINE LONDON	14/8	1/10	-/11	-/5½	2/6
BEST (High Strength) Sweetened or Unsweetened	17/4	2/2	1/1	-/6½	3/-
GINGER	16/-	2/-	1/-	-/6	2/10
SLOE	17/4	2/2	1/1	-/6½	
HOLLANDS—FINEST SCHIEDAM	18/-	2/4	1/2	-/7	3/4

WINES. (BY IMPERIAL MEASURE.)

	Per Gal.	Per Pint.	Per ½-Pt.	Per ¼-Pt.	Per Bot.
PORT—GOOD FRUITY DINNER WINE	11/4	1/5	-/8½	-/4½	2/-
FINEST OLD, CHARACTER OF BOTTLED WINE	16/-	2/-	1/-	-/6	2/10
SHERRY—GOOD DINNER WINE	9/4	1/2	-/7	-/3½	1/8
SUPERIOR OLD	16/	2/-	1/-	-/6	2/10

PORTS per Bottle		1/8	2/-	2/6	2/10 3/6 4/- &c.
SHERRIES ditto	1/4	1/8	2/-	2/2 2/4	2/6 2/10 3/- 3/4 &c.
SPANISH PORT per Bottle					1/- 1/4
CLARET ditto		10d	1/-	1/3 1/6	2/- 3/- 4/-
Ditto	per Half Bottle	8d	10d	1/4 2/-	&c.
AUSTRALIAN BURGUNDY, per Bottle					1/3
Ditto ditto	per Half Bottle				9d
BURGUNDY per Bottle				1/6	2/- &c.
HOCK ditto				1/6	2/- &c.
SAUTERNE ditto	1/4	2/-	2/6	3/-	&c.
CHAMPAGNE ditto	2/10	3/2	3/8	4/8 5/2	5/8 &c.
Ditto Quarter Bottles 1/- 2/-	Half Bottles 1/7	2/-	2/7	3/-	3/1 3/9 &c.

ALES. (BY IMPERIAL MEASURE.)

	Per Gal.	Per Pint	Per Bottle.
BASS & CO.'S ALES MILD	1/4	-/2	
STRONG	1/8	-/2½	
BEST BITTER	2/-	-/3	-/3½ imperial pint
	—	-/2	imperial ½-pint
OLD, EXTRA STRENGTH	2/8	-/4	-/4½ imperial pint
			-/2½ imperial ½-pint
WORTHINGTON'S DINNER ALE			-/2½ imperial pint

1852 All was far from calm and bright on Boxing Day 1852, as this report from a Cheltenham newspaper of the time tells us. 'Severe storm, during which windows were blown in and chimneys blown down in every direction. In Suffolk Lawn one of the large ornamental trees was blown down, and another at Dr. Barnard's, Cambray shared the same fate. A long range of stabling in the Royal Hotel yard was destroyed and in the Bath Road a poor woman was blown completely off her feet, and hurled with considerable violence into the middle of the road.'

26 December

1936 Edgar Piper was a familiar figure to animal lovers in the county during the 1920s and 1930s. He operated a mobile pet shop, towed behind his tricycle, which sold birds, small animals and food for both. 'Piper's performing birds' was an act much in demand for children's parties and charity shows. A dapper chap in wing-collar shirt and evening suit, Edgar put his well-trained budgies through their paces. His feathered friends performed tricks on see-saws, roundabouts and mini fair-ground rides, all of which Mr Piper made himself.

Tragedy struck this cruel day when Edgar was parked in the Promenade, Cheltenham. One of his tortoises made a dash for freedom, and was run over by a passing car.

27 December

Bishops Cleeve's senior citizens at the annual Christmas tea in the skittle alley of the Royal Oak, 1937. 'It's the high spot of our year,' one pensioner said.

Leckhampton churchyard.

1862 Fog was the problem this chilly morning when a Charlton Kings butcher named Attewell lost his way in the pea-souper and drove his gig into a deep pond. 'Mr. Attwell was got out without serious injury' a report of the time informs us, 'but the horse drowned.'

A story from the collective memory of villagers at Marshfield recalls a local hatter named Billy Oakel, whose wife possessed special powers. She used tarot cards to tell fortunes, but more unusually was apparently able to freeze people in their tracks by pointing at them with a stick.

It seems likely that Mr and Mrs Oakel's marriage was not one made in heaven. When Billy died, neighbours noticed that his wife had dragged his corpse out of the house and was giving it a good thrashing with a broom. When asked why she was doing this, she replied that he had beaten her often enough when he was alive, and this was the opportunity she had been waiting for to get her own back.

The most ancient Gloucestershire tale of witches and witchcraft dates from pre-Norman Conquest times. It concerns the Witch of Berkeley, who learned in a vision that she was about to die and so took vigorous steps to prevent the Devil from claiming her soul. She instructed her son, who was a monk, and her daughter, a nun, to kill a stag and wrap her dead body in the skin of the animal. Then she asked them to deposit her corpse in a stone coffin, secure the lid with three iron chains, and position it in the local church with the door locked.

On the first night the Devil broke into the church and worked all night to break one of the chains before daybreak. The second night he did the same again. You may, dear reader, at this point be thinking that a twist to the story will save the deceased witch from Old Nick's clutches. But not a bit of it. On the third night the Devil broke into the church once more, snapped the remaining chain and, having impaled the corpse on a meat-hook attached to the saddle of his black steed, galloped off with his prize to the underworld.

An old Forest of Dean saying: 'Death is the one thing we've all got to look forward to, if we do live long enough.'

BIBLIOGRAPHY

Dixon, Reginald, *Cotswold Curiosities*, Dovecote Press, 1988

Donaldson, D.N., *Winchcombe: A History of the Cotswold Borough*, Wychwood Press, 2001

Duncan, Michael, *Underground from Posen*, William Kimber, 1954

Gloucestershire Federation of Women's Institutes, *Gloucestershire within Living Memory*, Countryside Books, 1996

Household, Humphrey, *Thames and Severn Canal*, Alan Sutton, 1983

Moody, Raymond, *Burford: An Introduction and Guide*, 2001

Moore, Ann, *Gloucestershire Past*, Alan Sutton, 1995

Norman's History of Cheltenham, John Goding, 1863

One Road to Imjin, Dew Line Publications

Palmer, Roy, *Folklore of Gloucestershire*, Tempus, 2001

Smith, Betty, *Tales of Old Gloucestershire*, Countryside Books, 1987

The Citizen

Gloucestershire Echo

Gloucester Journal